T0041251

THE
ESSENTIAL
VEGETARIAN
AIR FRYER
COOKBOOK

THE ESSENTIAL

VEGETARIAN

AIR FRYER

COOKBOOK

75+ EASY MEATLESS RECIPES

LINDA LARSEN

PHOTOGRAPHY BY DARREN MUIR

ROCKRIDGE PRESS

Copyright © 2020 by Rockridge Press, Emeryville, California

No part of this publication may be reproduced, stored in a retrieval system, or transmitted in any form or by any means, electronic, mechanical, photocopying, recording, scanning, or otherwise, except as permitted under Sections 107 or 108 of the 1976 United States Copyright Act, without the prior written permission of the Publisher. Requests to the Publisher for permission should be addressed to the Permissions Department, Rockridge Press, 6005 Shellmound Street, Suite 175, Emeryville, CA 94608.

Limit of Liability/Disclaimer of Warranty: The Publisher and the author make no representations or warranties with respect to the accuracy or completeness of the contents of this work and specifically disclaim all warranties, including without limitation warranties of fitness for a particular purpose. No warranty may be created or extended by sales or promotional materials. The advice and strategies contained herein may not be suitable for every situation. This work is sold with the understanding that the Publisher is not engaged in rendering medical, legal, or other professional advice or services. If professional assistance is required, the services of a competent professional person should be sought. Neither the Publisher nor the author shall be liable for damages arising herefrom. The fact that an individual, organization, or website is referred to in this work as a citation and/or potential source of further information does not mean that the author or the Publisher endorses the information the individual, organization, or website may provide or recommendations they/it may make. Further, readers should be aware that websites listed in this work may have changed or disappeared between when this work was written and when it is read.

For general information on our other products and services or to obtain technical support, please contact our Customer Care Department within the United States at (866) 744-2665, or outside the United States at (510) 253-0500.

Rockridge Press publishes its books in a variety of electronic and print formats. Some content that appears in print may not be available in electronic books, and vice versa.

TRADEMARKS: Rockridge Press and the Rockridge Press logo are trademarks or registered trademarks of Callisto Media Inc. and/or its affiliates, in the United States and other countries, and may not be used without written permission. All other trademarks are the property of their respective owners. Rockridge Press is not associated with any product or vendor mentioned in this book.

Interior and Cover Designer: Karmen Lizzul
Art Producer: Hannah Dickerson
Editors: Daniel Grogan and Bridget Fitzgerald
Production Editor: Mia Moran
Photography © Darren Muir 2020
Author photo courtesy of Picture This Northfield

ISBN: Print 978-1-64611-535-8 | eBook 978-1-64611-536-5
R0

I dedicate this book to my dear husband,
Doug; my beautiful nieces, Maddie and Grace;
and my wonderful nephew, Michael.
They are a joy and a delight!

CONTENTS

INTRODUCTION

I am in love with the air fryer. I say that unabashedly and with no remorse. This countertop appliance has changed the way I cook. And you'll feel the same after just a few uses. This is my fourth air fryer book, and I don't see a limit on how many I can write, since the air fryer has almost unlimited potential to cook just about every recipe in the world.

The air fryer was introduced about 10 years ago as a replacement for unhealthy, messy, time-consuming, harrowing, and high-calorie deep-frying. The swirling hot air inside the appliance mimics cooking food in hot oil, but with no muss and fuss. Imagine: You can "fry" carrots and zucchini to make crisp fries and not have to worry about disposing of a quart of oil. The air fryer produces food with the same look, texture, and taste of deep-fried foods, but with very little fat and much fewer calories. What's not to love?

But that's not all the air fryer can do. As the appliance evolved and changed to incorporate timed cooking and preset temperatures, people discovered its versatility. The air fryer can replace your stovetop, oven, and grill. You can sauté, steam, simmer, stir-fry, bake, roast, and grill just about any food in your air fryer. And its compact size and easy cleanup are bonuses.

Most of the recipes you may have seen for the air fryer are for foods such as fried chicken, chicken nuggets, and chicken wings. But you don't have to be a meat-eater to use the air fryer; vegetarian foods are delicious cooked in this appliance. Every vegetarian and vegan recipe I know of, with few exceptions, can be cooked in the air fryer. You don't have to limit yourself to grilled tofu or stove-top beans and rice.

If you are a dedicated vegetarian, you already know this: Vegetarian recipes are incredibly diverse. Plant foods are not only nutritious, colorful, and healthy, they are delicious, especially when cooked in the air fryer. You can use your air fryer to make veggie sandwiches and quesadillas, pasta sauces and risotto, and even bread, pancakes, brownies, and pies. The possibilities are endless.

Because the air fryer is so easy to use, you'll want to try recipes that perhaps didn't fit into your diet until now. Have you heard of Buffalo Cauliflower, the vegetarian equivalent to Buffalo wings? This deep-fried treat is actually healthy when air fried. Warm vegetable salads are a snap to make in the air fryer. And if you aren't yet a committed vegetarian, the air fryer is a great way to easily add more veggies and fruits into your diet. This type of cooking will also make it easier for new vegetarians to make the transition from burgers and chicken to more healthy and interesting foods made without meat—because the food turns out perfectly every time.

The recipes in this book focus on fresh and whole ingredients that are easy to find in any grocery store. You won't need to make a trip to a specialty store or order something online to make the recipes in this book, but you can still incorporate flavors, foods, and spices from every cuisine around the world. You'll find Tex-Mex treats, recipes from Thailand and other Asian countries, American classics, foods from Italy and Spain, and some surprises that fuse several cuisines in one recipe. I chose these foods to not only show you how versatile the air fryer is, but to highlight how diverse and adaptable a vegetarian diet can be. Join me and let's cook!

CHAPTER ONE

AIR FRYER
BASICS

If you've never used an air fryer before, you are in for a treat. If you're an experienced pro, you can dive right into the recipes. The air fryer can turn vegetables into crisp chips and fries; it can roast them to tender perfection to add to soups or salads; it can transform fruits into crisps and cakes; and it can even turn leftovers into fabulous snacks. This little R2-D2–shaped appliance has a powerful heater and fan that make quick work of just about any recipe you can think of.

THE VEGETARIAN ADVANTAGE

Vegetarian cooking is so easy and simple in the air fryer for several reasons. First of all, air-fried food is healthier. If you make zucchini chips or kale chips in an air fryer, they will be incredibly crunchy, crisp, and yet tender with very little oil. All you need to do is spritz a bit of oil on the food and the machine does all the work. Air fryer recipes are also faster than traditional recipes, whether you are frying, roasting, baking, or stir-frying. The machine heats up very quickly, so you aren't waiting for a pot of oil on the stove to reach the correct temperature or killing time until a big cavernous oven preheats to 400°F. Here are a few more benefits of vegetarian air frying:

Healthy Air-fried food is healthier. There's no comparison between deep-frying and air frying, but let's compare anyway. Most "fried" foods cooked in the air fryer have 80 percent fewer fat grams and calories than foods cooked in the deep fat fryer. So, these recipes are heart-healthy, as well.

Easy How many times have you had to clean your oven because something spattered or overflowed or just made a mess? And how many times have you stood at the stove stirring food that's cooking in a wok, pot, or pan? With the air fryer, just put food into the basket and slide it into the machine. You may have to shake the basket once or twice during cooking, but that's it. And cleanup is so simple. All of the moving components are nonstick and many are dishwasher safe.

Fast Convection cooking, in which a fan moves the hot air around, cooks about 30 percent faster than conventional cooking. That means the food is ready in a flash. The food cooks more evenly, too, since the moving hot air cooks every inch of it evenly.

Versatile If one member of your family wants to have steamed asparagus, while another wants a cheese and veggie quesadilla, you can cook them both in the air fryer. The only thing that will change for each recipe is the time and temperature. You may need to wipe out the basket with a paper towel between recipes, but that's it. The air fryer can handle it all.

HOW IT WORKS

The air fryer is a compact appliance that is very powerful. It's actually a countertop convection oven.

Air fryer components include the casing, a control panel, a heating element, a fan, and a basket to hold the food. Food cooks more quickly in the air fryer for three reasons: (1) The fan moves hot air around the food, which speeds up the cooking process; (2) because the cooking area is so compact, with not much space inside, the heat is intensified; and (3) the basket is perforated, which means the hot air comes into direct contact with the food. Although deep-frying cooks food a little more quickly once it's in the oil, with an air fryer you don't need to wait 15 to 20 minutes for the oil to come to temperature before you can start cooking.

Air frying, like deep-frying, is a dry-heat cooking method. That may sound surprising, because deep-frying uses liquid oil, but "dry heat" simply means no water is used to cook the food. Hot oil is a very good heat conductor, but so is hot air when it is moving. Both cooking methods remove water from the surface of food. Once the water is gone, the Maillard effect begins. This effect means the proteins and sugars on the surface of food heat up, which breaks them down into smaller molecules. Those molecules recombine to produce flavor compounds and that nice golden brown color.

The air fryer produces food that is crisp and golden brown, while still remaining juicy and tender on the inside. The deep fryer does the same thing, but takes more work, since you have to add the oil and then somehow get rid of it—not to mention watching the food carefully while it cooks so it doesn't burn. The air fryer is also much safer than a deep fryer. Quarts of boiling oil are a real kitchen hazard; I've actually had nightmares about it!

Crowd-pleasing If you're serving a crowd at a party or for dinner, the air fryer can handle it. Larger air fryers, with a 6-quart basket, can hold 2 pounds of French fries and cook them to crisp perfection in just 15 to 20 minutes. Baking those fries in the oven (after you've waited for the oven to preheat) takes 45 minutes. And they'll only be crisp if you're lucky! Using a rack to double up inside the air fryer pan lets you cook a side dish and main dish at the same time. Try doing that in a microwave oven.

Taste Air frying and roasting bring out the wonderful flavors of vegetables. The sugars in the foods caramelize and combine with proteins in the high, dry heat, which produces many flavor compounds that are simply delicious. The texture of veggies cooked in the air fryer is also wonderful, with crisp and crunchy exteriors and soft and melting interiors.

CHOOSING YOUR FRYER

There are many different air fryer models on the market, with more being added every year. The one you choose depends on a few factors. The way you cook will help you determine which air fryer to buy. Think about what you like to cook and the number of people you cook for.

All the Features

The air fryer basket capacity is the most important feature to consider when determining which model to buy. Various models have baskets that range from 2 to 5.8 quarts. If you are cooking for one or two people, you can choose the smaller size. But if you cook for a family or have lots of parties, choose an air fryer with larger capacity so you don't have to cook the food in multiple batches.

Most air fryers have a temperature range of 100°F to 400°F. Most foods cook in the 350°F to 400°F range. All air fryers reach temperature quickly, usually within just a few minutes. Some air fryers will need these few minutes to preheat whereas others can simply be set to the correct temperature.

The simplest air fryers have a control panel that lets you select the cooking time and temperature. But some models have programmable functions and even preset functions, such as French Fry, that let you cook at the touch of a button. Another function can delay cooking up to 4 hours, and some air fryers are even enabled with Wi-Fi so you can start the appliance without even being in the same room!

I have three air fryers (big surprise!) that I love. I have the Ninja 5.5 quart, the GoWISE 3.7 quart, and the Philips TurboStar, which is 2.75 quarts. I use them all, depending on what I am cooking and the number of people I am feeding. I used all of them to develop the recipes in this book.

Fryer Choices

The top five air fryer brands offer many different choices with different capacities and features, at many different price points. These are the best.

1   **Philips TurboStar Technology Airfryer** This machine is smaller than most, even though the basket holds up to 1.8 pounds of food. Its digital controls are simple to use and intuitive. It also heats up instantly and has a Keep Warm function.

2   **GoWISE USA 5.8-Quart 8-in-1 Air Fryer** This inexpensive machine is a real workhorse. It's a programmable machine with eight presets. A Start/Stop button lets you change the time and temperature in the middle of a cooking cycle.

3   **Ninja 4-Quart Air Fryer** This classic model will cook up to 2 pounds of food in one session. The panel lets you choose air fry, reheat, roast, or dehydrate. It does take a few minutes to get to cooking temperature.

4   **Nuwave Brio 6-Quart Digital Air Fryer** This machine can cook 3 pounds of French fries in one batch. It includes a basket divider so you can cook two foods at the same time.

5   **BLACK+DECKER PuriFry Air Fryer** This smaller machine is perfect for small families. It has dual convection fans to cook food quickly, with a 2-liter capacity. It's simple and easy to use.

REMOVING PANS FROM THE AIR FRYER

When air fryers were first introduced, people used them to cook fries and heat up pizza. But as more people developed more complex recipes, including cakes and breads, a problem arose: How do you get a cake pan or a cookie sheet out of the air fryer basket without burning yourself? Most of these accessories fit very closely in the basket with not a lot of room, and you can't just turn the basket over to remove a delicate cake.

There are a few solutions. One is to make a foil sling. First, measure the bottom and sides of the inside of your air fryer basket and add them together. Tear off a piece of heavy-duty aluminum foil as long as the number you just totaled. Fold it in half lengthwise, then in half again to make a long strip. Put the sling in the air fryer basket so it goes down one side, across the bottom, and up the other side. Then, put the cake pan or cookie sheet on top. When the food is done, put oven mitts on your hands or use two tongs and grab the foil to lift the pan out. The foil will be hot! You can also use this sling to lower a pan containing cake batter into the air fryer.

Another solution is to use something called a plate gripper or plate clip, which you can find online. It looks like a strange pair of tongs with two triangular wire legs. It is used often by caterers to lift plates out of boiling water. You position the ends of the legs under the plate or cookie sheet, then squeeze the top so you can lift it straight out of the basket. Some air fryer accessory kits now include this tool.

Silicone-tipped tongs are another useful tool. You can grip the sides of a pan (as long as it isn't filled to the brim) and remove it from the basket. Two tongs work well to pull a pan out of the air fryer.

Finally, something called a cake barrel may be what you need. This is a fairly deep 6- or 7-inch round pan that has a hinged metal handle on top. You can easily lift the pan out of the basket with the handle, using oven mitts.

GET STARTED

Now that you've considered the available models and chosen the air fryer that will work best for your needs, it's time to put it to use. Once you get your air fryer home, unpack it and get ready to make some fabulous food. Let's walk through step-by-step instructions, and I'll give you my top tips that will help you get the most out of this convenient appliance.

Step by Step

The first thing you should do when you open your air fryer is read the instruction booklet. Even if you've owned an air fryer before, read every word. Each machine may have different warnings and safety concerns. You need to know how your air fryer works.

Clean the machine before the first use. Wipe down the outside with a damp paper towel. Rinse out the basket and dry it thoroughly. If the air fryer came with accessories, clean those, too.

The air fryer should be set on a solid, heatproof surface. Watch out for overhanging cabinets. Most air fryers need a clearance space of 5 inches on all sides—that means 5 inches of space to the back, sides, front, and top. The appliance emits steam as it works and that steam has to escape so the food can crisp. Here's another safety warning: The steam that comes out of the air fryer will be hot. Stay away from it while the machine is working.

Some air fryers require a short preheating time of a few minutes; others do not. Read that instruction manual to get specifics for your machine.

One of the most important tips to get the most out of your air fryer lies in food preparation. Foods should be cut to about the same size, so they cook evenly for the same amount of time. Pat foods dry and spritz with a little oil if the recipe calls for it (see "On Oil" on page 14 for more information). You can find oil misters in most supermarkets or cooking supply stores.

Remove the basket from the air fryer (be careful if the air fryer has preheated because the basket will be hot!) and add the food. Most foods cook best when placed in a single layer, but some foods can be piled into the basket. Follow the recipe instructions. Or you may use a raised rack and put some food in the basket itself and some on the rack, which fits snugly into the basket.

Set the time and temperature and stand back! Take this time to clean up, get serving dishes and bowls ready, or just sit back and relax. You may need to remove and shake the basket once or twice during the cooking time or rearrange the food. Use an oven mitt or potholder and be careful!

When you remove the food from the air fryer, pull the basket out. It's best not to overturn the basket onto the dish or bowl, since oil that drips down from some food could spill over the food (or your hand). Use a pair of silicone-tipped tongs to remove the food. Put the basket back into the air fryer, turn it off, unplug it, and dig in.

Top Tips

These are the tips and tricks for using the air fryer that work best for me; pick and choose your favorites depending on what you cook.

» Unless the recipe says you can load up the basket, limit the amount of food you place in it. Most foods need a bit of space around each piece so the air can circulate. This tip also applies to deep-frying; if you add too much food at once, it won't cook evenly.

» Don't use a liquid or very wet batter to coat the food. Deep-fried foods can be coated with a runny batter because the hot oil immediately sets it upon contact. Air isn't as good a conductor of heat as oil is, so batters take a minute or two to set, and in the meantime they drip all over—something you want to avoid in an air fryer.

» Don't cut food too small. Most veggies should be at least ¼ inch wide so they don't fall through the holes or perforations in the basket.

» If you're cooking light foods such as kale chips, use a small metal trivet with legs to weigh the food down so it doesn't fly around inside the basket.

» Don't add a lot of oil to the food you're cooking. The oil will drip off, making a mess. Additionally, a lot of oil will prevent the crispness we all crave.

» Make sure you clean your air fryer after every use. Any oil or food debris left behind can oxidize and will make your food taste rancid. Ick!

FAQs

QUESTION	ANSWER
What do I do if my air fryer is smoking?	If the air fryer is emitting white smoke, the food is too fatty. Turn it off, remove the basket, take out the food, and carefully drain off the excess oil. Black smoke means something is wrong. Unplug the appliance and take it to a repair shop.
Why isn't my food getting crispy?	If your food isn't crisp, the basket is probably over-crowded. Remove some of the food and cook for a few minutes longer. Shake the basket once to promote even cooking. The food could also be too wet; pat it dry with paper towels and resume cooking for a few minutes.
Why isn't the food browning?	The food may be too wet; pat with paper towels to remove moisture. Or there may not be enough oil on the food; add a bit of oil with your oil mister.
Why are season-ings like herbs and spices and bread-ing coming off the food as it cooks?	Light and tiny ingredients such as dried herbs can fly around in the air fryer. Spray food with a bit of oil before you add the herbs, so they stick to the food. Same with bread crumbs; press them onto the food firmly so they stick.
Why is my food cooking unevenly?	Uneven cooking means the basket is overcrowded. Remove some of the food and cook in two batches. You can also prevent uneven cooking by shaking the basket or rearranging the food halfway through cooking time.
Why is the coating on the metal basket starting to chip?	Never use nonstick baking or cooking sprays on the basket. They contain chemicals that can damage the nonstick coating. If that happens, replace the basket.

AIR-FRIED FLEXIBILITY

You know by now that the air fryer can "fry" foods so they taste like they were deep-fried. Who wouldn't love a crispy carrot or sweet potato fry? But this versatile appliance can do more than you think—especially with some basic air fryer accessories such as a baking pan, cake barrel (see page 6), metal bowl, or cookie sheet.

Roasting You can roast foods in your air fryer. To roast foods, they must be cooked at a high temperature in dry heat. You won't believe how good roasted broccoli or cauliflower is when it's sprayed with a little oil and sprinkled with seasonings. Roasting brings out the sweetness and flavor in vegetables while browning and crisping the surface. Even people who are lukewarm about vegetables will love them cooked this way.

Baking You can bake foods in your air fryer. Make muffins, donuts, brownies, cookies, tartlets, cakes, breads, pizzas, and whole potatoes in this appliance. You'll need to use a pan or insert to cook these foods, but those are readily available online. These baked goods will have crisp and brown crusts and fluffy and tender interiors. A pizza will be crisp and browned, with tender toppings, and breads will be beautifully browned, and moist and tender inside.

Grilling Use your air fryer to grill veggies and foods, such as quesadillas and tofu steaks. A grill pan that fits inside the air fryer basket can make grill marks just like your outdoor gas or electric grill. Adding a bit of liquid smoke to the food before you cook it adds a smoky flavor. You can even make grilled sandwiches and vegetable kabobs.

. . . and more! Try making a stir-fry in this appliance. A metal bowl or pan placed in the basket acts just like a wok. You'll need to stir the food once or twice while it's cooking, but it's so much easier to stir-fry in the air fryer than on the stovetop.

Casserole-type foods also cook well in the air fryer. You can make mac and cheese, bread pudding, risotto, and grain bowls in minutes.

The air fryer caramelizes vegetables beautifully. Veggies that caramelize have high sugar content, including carrots, onions, beets, and parsnips. Caramelized vegetables are crisp and browned, with a delicious sweet taste. They are perfect for getting your family excited about veggies.

TIPS FOR MAKING THE AIR FRYER WORK FOR YOU

All vegetables cook well in the air fryer, whether you are roasting, grilling, frying, or baking them. You can use both fresh and frozen vegetables in this appliance; the only difference will be in the timing. Frozen veggies will take less time to cook because they are already softened.

Cheese melts beautifully in the air fryer, but don't add it to the fryer on its own. It's delicious on pizza, in casseroles, and in sandwiches. You can cook the cheese until it melts, or until it browns and gets kind of crusty. Both are delicious. By the way, hardboiled eggs are fabulous cooked in this appliance.

Foods that don't work as well in the air fryer include anything with a liquidy or wet batter. Remember that those wet batters will drop off the food before they set, making a mess.

Don't put whole vegetables such as large carrots, parsnips, large whole onions, or other big root vegetables into the air fryer. They will take a long time to soften, and the exterior may burn before the inside is done. Cut the veggies into smaller pieces for best results. However, a whole baked potato, pricked with a fork before cooking, is a wonderful thing in the air fryer.

THE VEGGIE KITCHEN

A well-stocked kitchen—pantry, refrigerator, and freezer—and a good strategy can make your cooking much faster and easier.

Think about the foods you like to cook, and your family likes to eat. It's a good idea to keep the ingredients for several favorite recipes on hand at all times so you can make a delicious meal at the drop of a hat. It's also a good idea to plan out your meals for the week ahead before you shop. You'll feel more secure if you know you can get food on the table in a hurry.

Staples

These staples are foods that everyone should have in their kitchen. With them, you can cook many recipes without having to go to the store—another time-saving bonus!

Pantry basics It's always good to have flour, dried bread crumbs, panko bread crumbs, rice, baking powder, baking soda, pasta, oatmeal, dried cranberries, brown and granulated sugars, peanut butter, honey, and chocolate chips in stock.

Nuts and seeds These ingredients add texture and flavor to your recipes. Stock pecans, sesame seeds, and walnuts.

Canned beans This staple should always be in your vegetarian pantry. You can stock black beans, pinto beans, cannellini beans, chickpeas (garbanzo beans), and red beans.

Canned goods Keep vegetable broth, coconut milk, canned tomatoes, and tomato paste on hand.

Tofu Every vegetarian kitchen needs tofu in several forms. Buy the shelf-stable variety that doesn't need refrigeration. Tofu varieties you'll use in the air fryer include firm, extra-firm, and super firm.

Cheeses Keep a good variety of cheeses on hand, including Parmesan, Cheddar, Swiss, provolone, and pepper Jack.

Root vegetables The air fryer makes quick work of onions, garlic, potatoes, and sweet potatoes, making them tender and crisp.

Other vegetables Staple vegetables include fresh mushrooms, bell peppers, chiles, cauliflower, and cabbage.

Frozen vegetables Frozen broccoli, peas, corn, spinach, sliced carrots, green beans, and squash all cook beautifully in the air fryer.

Fruits You should always have apples on hand, as well as grapes and pears, and other fruits you know your family likes.

Condiments Many of the recipes call for staple condiments such as soy sauce, mustard, ketchup, vinegar, oils, hoisin sauce, and barbecue sauce.

Frozen bread dough and puff pastry These staple items can be found in the frozen section of your grocery store. They will let you make fabulous breakfasts, appetizers, main dishes, and desserts in the air fryer.

Breads Most breads can be stored in the freezer or in your pantry, and are great to have on hand for sandwiches and appetizers.

Spices

The list of spices available in every grocery store is very long. But these are the herbs and spices that are used most often in this book. Of course, add your own favorites, as you can switch herbs and spices in most recipes to suit your taste.

Basil This herb has a slightly minty, smoky flavor and is essential for Italian recipes.

Chili powder This combination of several different spices is a shortcut for Mexican and Tex-Mex foods. You can buy it in mild and spicy forms.

Cinnamon Earthy and warm, cinnamon is used in many desserts and breakfast recipes, as well as to add a bit of spice to some main dishes.

Cumin This spice has an earthy and nutty flavor with hints of lemon; it's used in many cuisines and can sometimes substitute for red pepper flakes.

ON OIL

Not much oil is used when air frying, but it's important that you choose oils that will work well in this appliance. Most frying oils have little or no taste; they are used to make foods crisp and brown. The oil you choose will depend on your personal taste and how much you want to spend.

Since the air fryer cooks at such high temperatures, up to 400°F and even beyond, you'll need to use oils with higher smoke points. That point is the temperature at which the oil begins to break down and smoke, which can create unpleasant flavor compounds.

Oils with the highest smoke points include extra-light olive oil (not extra-virgin, with a smoke point of 380°F), soybean oil, canola oil, grape-seed oil, avocado oil, and peanut oil. The best way to use these oils with air-fried foods is to put them into a mister, which you can find online and at many baking and cooking supply stores.

You don't need to use oil when air frying food in most recipes, but oil is essential if you are adding fine seasonings, so they stick to the food. Some foods will be less crisp and brown without oil but will still be delicious. If you are skipping oil because of calorie concerns, please know that a spritz of oil contains about 2 calories. As well, some nutrients, especially vitamins A and D, are absorbed better by the body if you eat them with a bit of fat.

Store oil in a dark and cool place like your pantry, and use it within one year of the purchase date. Oil can oxidize and become rancid over time, which will add a very unpleasant taste to your food—plus, it isn't good for you.

Curry powder This is a blend of several different spices, including ginger, cinnamon, coriander, and pepper. Try several brands to see which one you like best. It can be mild or spicy.

Five-spice powder This is literally made up of five spices: cinnamon, star anise, fennel seeds, peppercorns, and cloves. It's essential for Asian recipes.

Ground ginger This pungent and warm spice is used in desserts and in main dishes.

Marjoram This herb is wonderful with milder vegetables such as carrots and potatoes, with a sweet and delicate flavor that isn't as spicy as oregano.

Nutmeg This intense spice is nutty and slightly sweet. It's used in dessert recipes.

Oregano Dried oregano is slightly bitter and aromatic, with a pungent flavor and aroma.

Paprika This spice is made from ground red peppers. You can find it in sweet, smoky, and hot forms.

Red pepper flakes This spicy pepper adds a lot of heat to recipes.

Salt and pepper These two essential spices are used in just about every recipe. Look for sea salt for intense flavor.

Thyme Dried thyme has a lemony flavor that is delicious with all vegetables.

Shopping and Meal Prep

If you're new to the vegetarian diet, or even if you're experienced, some planning is in order. Take a look at the staples and spice lists in this book and start preparing a shopping list. Add ingredients you don't have on hand. Then when you plan out your week, pull the recipes you want to make and create a shopping list.

Having a list when you are shopping is essential. Otherwise, you will buy more than you need, and you'll forget crucial ingredients for many recipes. Write your shopping list in the order of your favorite grocery store's layout. For instance, start with produce, work your way to dairy, then canned goods, and spices. Then follow the list and enjoy the process.

If you live in a multi-diet household, designate one refrigerator shelf for one eating plan and another shelf for another. In other words, put meat and poultry products on one shelf, and vegetarian products, such as tofu, on another. Meat and poultry should be on a lower shelf so juices don't drip onto produce.

Meal planning doesn't have to be difficult. Think about the foods you and your family like to eat and include those foods in your plan and shopping list weekly. Think about trying something new every once in a while, because it's good to introduce new foods and new tastes to your family diet. If you plan every week, make an efficient shopping list, and cook according to your plan, you can help minimize food waste. The vegetarian diet uses lots of fresh produce, so you want to use all the food before it spoils.

ABOUT THE RECIPES

These recipes were all developed to be delicious, simple to make, and healthy. Make sure you read the recipe start to finish before you begin cooking. The recipes all include nutritional information to help you make the best choices for your family. Some of the recipes need some air fryer accessories such as a pan, bowl, cookie sheet, or raised rack. Make sure you have all equipment on hand before you start cooking a recipe.

Labels

Every recipe will have a label that tells you a bit about it.

Fry/Bake/Grill/Roast This label tells you the technique used with the air fryer. Some air fryers have buttons that let you choose these cooking styles. But others simply indicate time and temperature.

5 Ingredients The recipe will only use five ingredients, not counting oil, salt, and pepper. There may be a tip added to the recipe so you can include another ingredient or two if you'd like.

30 Minutes The recipe can be prepared, with a little organization, in 30 minutes or less. That number includes preparation as well as cooking time.

Family-Friendly These recipes use common ingredients you can easily find at the grocery store, and you can be assured that every family member, including young children, will enjoy it.

Gluten-Free These recipes will not incorporate any ingredient that contains gluten, including pasta, breads, crackers, and wheat, barley, or rye flour.

Tips

Many of the recipes in this book include a tip that will help you with food preparation, the recipe itself, or cleanup.

Air Fryer Tip This tip will help you use the machine to its fullest capacity or adapt a recipe for different models.

Cooking Tip These tips will help make the dish easier to prepare, cook, or clean. You'll also get suggestions for shortcuts that will save time.

Ingredient Tip This tip gives you more information on selecting ingredients and working with them. It will also include helpful nutrition facts and places to buy the ingredient.

Substitution Tip This tip will provide acceptable and suitable substitutions for some of the ingredients in the recipe, such as using a different herb or spice.

Variation Tip These suggestions will help you try something new with the recipe or propose how to use leftovers.

Sweet Potato
Veggie Hash
PAGE 39

CHAPTER TWO

BREAKFASTS & BREADS

Apple Fritters

30 MINUTES, FAMILY-FRIENDLY / SERVES 4

PREP TIME:
15 minutes

COOK TIME:
10 minutes

FRY:
350°F

PER SERVING:
Calories: 318;
Protein: 5g;
Fat: 11g;
Saturated Fat: 6g;
Carbohydrates:
52g;
Sugar: 31g;
Sodium: 207g;
Fiber: 2g

Apple fritters are a combination of dough and fresh chopped apples that are typically deep-fried until crisp. The air fryer is a much better way to make this delicious breakfast recipe. The dough has to be thick enough so it doesn't flatten out when added to the air fryer basket, but thin enough so the fritters are tender. This recipe makes fritters that are the perfect texture: soft like a doughnut, but crisp on the outside like a cruller.

¾ cup all-purpose flour

2 tablespoons brown sugar

1 teaspoon baking powder

¼ teaspoon sea salt

½ teaspoon cinnamon

¼ cup 2% milk

1 large egg

3 teaspoons freshly squeezed orange juice, divided

1 Granny Smith apple, peeled, cored, and diced (see Tip)

3 tablespoons butter, melted, divided

⅔ cup powdered sugar

1 teaspoon vanilla

2 teaspoons grated orange zest

1 In a medium bowl, combine the flour, brown sugar, baking powder, salt, and cinnamon and mix well.

2 In a small bowl, whisk together the milk, egg, and 2 teaspoons of orange juice until combined. Stir this into the flour mixture.

3 Fold in the diced apples until they are evenly distributed.

4 Line the air fryer basket with parchment paper. Depending on the size of your air fryer, drop two ¼-cup measures of the fritter mixture onto the parchment paper, 1½ inches apart. Drizzle each fritter with ½ tablespoon of melted butter.

5 Set or preheat the air fryer to 350°F. Fry the fritters for 7 to 10 minutes or until they are golden brown and set. Remove from the air fryer and place on a cooling rack.

6 In a small bowl, combine the remaining 2 tablespoons of butter, powdered sugar, remaining 1 teaspoon of orange juice, and vanilla and blend well. Drizzle over the warm fritters. Sprinkle with the orange zest and serve.

SUBSTITUTION TIP: The apple used in this recipe should be fairly tart and firm enough to keep its shape in cooking. Good choices include Granny Smith, Braeburn, Jonagold, Honeycrisp, and Cortland.

Streusel Donuts

PREP TIME:
15 minutes

COOK TIME:
**6 minutes
per batch**

FRY:
350°F

PER SERVING:
Calories: 214;
Protein: 4g;
Fat: 9g;
Saturated Fat: 5g;
Carbohydrates:
30g;
Sugar: 14g;
Sodium: 113g;
Fiber: 1g

Homemade donuts are better than any donuts you can buy at a store. The aroma as these donuts are "frying" is incredible. And the streusel—the sweet, crumbly topping—adds more interest and some delicious crunch. You can make the dough ahead of time and refrigerate it; then roll it out, cut out the donuts, top with the streusel, and fry.

1 cup plus 2 tablespoons all-purpose flour, divided, plus additional to dust the work surface

5 tablespoons dark brown sugar, divided

1 teaspoon baking powder

Pinch sea salt

¼ cup whole milk

1 large egg, yolk and white separated

3 tablespoons granulated sugar

½ teaspoon ground cinnamon

¼ cup butter, melted

Cooking oil spray

1 In a medium bowl, combine 1 cup of flour, 2 tablespoons of brown sugar, the baking powder, and salt and mix well.

2 In a small bowl, whisk together the milk and egg yolk. Add this to the flour mixture and mix just until a dough forms.

3 In another small bowl, combine the remaining 3 tablespoons of brown sugar, granulated sugar, cinnamon, remaining 2 tablespoons of flour, and butter and mix until a crumbly streusel forms Set aside.

4 Dust the work surface with some flour. Turn the dough out onto the surface and pat it to ⅓-inch thickness. Using a 3-inch cookie cutter, cut out 6 rounds. We'll skip the donut holes so we can have more streusel on top.

5 Beat the egg white until frothy in a small bowl, then brush the tops of the rounds with some of the egg white.

6 Sprinkle each dough round with some of the streusel topping, patting the topping onto the dough so it sticks.

7 Cut two pieces of parchment paper to fit in your air fryer basket. Place a parchment paper round into the air fryer basket and add the donuts, three at a time, depending on the size of your air fryer. Spray the tops with cooking oil.

8 Set or preheat the air fryer to 350°F. Fry the donuts for 4 to 6 minutes or until they are light golden brown. Remove and cool on a wire rack. Remove and discard the parchment paper and replace with a fresh round. Air fry the remaining donuts.

Nutty French Toast

PREP TIME:
15 minutes

COOK TIME:
**9 minutes
per batch**

BAKE:
350°F

_____

PER SERVING:
Calories: 475;
Protein: 11g;
Fat: 31g;
Saturated Fat: 11g;
Carbohydrates:
41g;
Sugar: 22g;
Sodium: 346g;
Fiber: 3g

French toast doesn't have to be plain. In this recipe, the bread slices are dipped into an egg-milk mixture as usual, but are then dipped into cinnamon-dusted pecans. The pecans toast as the French toast cooks, making a fragrant and memorable breakfast dish.

2 large eggs

⅔ cup whole milk

1 teaspoon vanilla

4 slices French bread

⅓ cup packed brown sugar

¼ cup butter

⅔ cup chopped pecans

¼ teaspoon cinnamon

1 In a large, shallow bowl, whisk together the eggs, milk, and vanilla until smooth.

2 Place the French bread slices into the bowl and let sit for 1 minute. Then turn the bread and let sit until you're ready to cook.

3 In a small saucepan over low heat, combine the brown sugar and butter and heat until melted, stirring occasionally.

4 In a small bowl, toss the pecans with the cinnamon.

5 Remove the bread from the egg mixture and place in the air fryer basket; you may need to do this in two batches if you have a small air fryer. Drizzle the brown sugar mixture over the bread and top with the pecans.

6 Set or preheat the air fryer to 350°F. Bake for 7 to 9 minutes or until the French toast is golden brown and crisp. Serve.

Italian Frittata

30 MINUTES, FAMILY-FRIENDLY, GLUTEN-FREE / SERVES 3

PREP TIME:
15 minutes

COOK TIME:
15 minutes

BAKE:
350°F

PER SERVING:
Calories: 285;
Protein: 21g;
Fat: 21g;
Saturated Fat: 11g;
Carbohydrates: 5g;
Sugar: 3g;
Sodium: 515g;
Fiber: 1g

COOKING TIP:
Always use unsalted butter or solid shortening to grease pans when making baked goods. Greasing with salted butter makes the baked goods stick.

A frittata is sturdier than an omelet, but more tender than a strata. Eggs are cooked with onions and vegetables and some wonderful Italian herbs to make a breakfast that will see you through to lunch. It can be served room temperature or even cold, making it a great choice for breakfast on the run.

- **1 tablespoon unsalted butter, at room temperature**
- **4 large eggs, beaten**
- **¼ cup ricotta cheese**
- **¼ cup whole milk**
- **1 teaspoon dried Italian seasoning**
- **Pinch sea salt**
- **2 scallions, chopped**
- **1 garlic clove, minced**
- **⅓ cup chopped cherry tomatoes, drained**
- **½ cup shredded provolone cheese**
- **¼ cup grated Parmesan cheese**

1 Grease a 7-inch round pan with the butter and set aside.

2 In a medium bowl, beat the eggs with the ricotta, milk, Italian seasoning, and salt. Pour this into the prepared pan.

3 Arrange the scallions, garlic, and tomatoes on the eggs. Top with the cheeses.

4 Set or preheat the air fryer to 350°F. Put the pan in the basket and the basket in the air fryer. Cook for 12 to 15 minutes or until the eggs are set and puffed. Serve.

SUBSTITUTION TIP: Use other cooked vegetables in this recipe. Try using leftover cooked chopped asparagus, cooked chopped red bell peppers, or cooked broccoli florets.

Pesto Omelet

30 MINUTES, FAMILY-FRIENDLY, GLUTEN-FREE / SERVES 3

PREP TIME:
15 minutes

COOK TIME:
15 minutes

BAKE:
350°F

PER SERVING:
Calories: 308;
Protein: 15g;
Fat: 25g;
Saturated Fat: 8g;
Carbohydrates: 8g;
Sugar: 2g;
Sodium: 565g;
Fiber: 1g

INGREDIENT TIP:
You can buy pesto, but it's easy to make your own. Combine 1 cup fresh basil leaves, ¼ cup grated Parmesan cheese, ¼ cup pine nuts, 3 tablespoons extra-virgin olive oil, 2 garlic cloves, a pinch of sea salt, and freshly ground black pepper in a food processor.

This omelet is cooked with vegetables and finished with fragrant basil pesto for a delicious breakfast treat. The vegetables are cooked in the air fryer first, then the egg mixture is added and cooked until puffy and light. Be sure everyone is ready and waiting to eat the omelet when it's hot and ethereal.

1 tablespoon olive oil	4 large eggs
1 shallot, minced	2 tablespoons light cream
1 garlic clove, minced	¼ teaspoon sea salt
½ cup diced red bell pepper	½ cup shredded mozzarella cheese
¼ cup chopped fresh tomato	3 tablespoons basil pesto

1 In a 6-inch round pan, place the olive oil. Add the shallot, garlic, bell pepper, and tomato and toss to coat in the oil.

2 Set or preheat the air fryer to 350°F. Put the pan with the vegetables in the basket and the basket in the air fryer. Cook for 3 to 5 minutes, stirring once halfway through cooking time, until the veggies are tender.

3 Meanwhile, whisk together the eggs, cream, and salt until smooth.

4 When the vegetables are done, remove the basket. Pour the egg mixture into the pan. Return the basket to the air fryer and cook for 8 minutes.

5 Sprinkle with the cheese and cook another 2 minutes or until the cheese is melted and the eggs are set. Top with the pesto and serve immediately.

Cranberry Oatmeal Muffins

30 MINUTES, FAMILY-FRIENDLY / SERVES 4

PREP TIME:
15 minutes

COOK TIME:
14 minutes

BAKE:
325°F

PER SERVING:
Calories: 232;
Protein: 5g;
Fat: 9g;
Saturated Fat: 1g;
Carbohydrates:
32g;
Sugar: 14g;
Sodium: 85g;
Fiber: 2g

COOKING TIP:
A muffin tin is usually too big for the air fryer basket; you need something that will stand on its own. Reusable silicone muffin cups are a good purchase if you want to make muffins often in the air fryer. You can also use aluminum foil muffin cups lined with parchment paper.

Fresh muffins, warm from the air fryer, are a great addition to any breakfast, as well as a wonderful snack. These muffins are made with oatmeal, which makes them very tender and moist, and dried cranberries, which add a great sweet and tart flavor. Serve them warm with some soft butter.

½ cup all-purpose flour

2 tablespoons
whole-wheat flour

½ teaspoon baking powder

2 tablespoons brown sugar

3 tablespoons
quick-cooking oats

Pinch sea salt

1 large egg

¼ cup whole milk

1 teaspoon vanilla

2 tablespoons vegetable oil

⅓ cup dried cranberries

Nonstick baking spray
containing flour

1 In a medium bowl, combine the all-purpose and whole-wheat flours, baking powder, brown sugar, oats, and salt and mix.

2 In a small bowl or a measuring cup, beat together the egg, milk, vanilla, and oil until combined.

3 Add the egg mixture to the dry ingredients all at once and stir just until combined.

4 Stir in the cranberries.

5 Spray four silicone muffin cups with the baking spray. Divide the batter among them, filling each two-thirds full.

6 Set or preheat the air fryer to 325°F. Place the muffin cups in the air fryer basket and the basket in the air fryer. Bake for 12 to 14 minutes or until the muffins are browned and the tops spring back when you touch them lightly with your finger.

7 Let the muffins cool on a wire rack for 10 to 15 minutes before serving.

Cottage Cheese German Pancakes

30 MINUTES, FAMILY-FRIENDLY / SERVES 3

PREP TIME:
15 minutes

COOK TIME:
15 minutes

BAKE:
375°F

PER SERVING:
Calories: 341;
Protein: 9g;
Fat: 21g;
Saturated Fat: 7g;
Carbohydrates: 31g;
Sugar: 19g;
Sodium: 190g;
Fiber: 2g

German Pancakes, also called Dutch Baby Pancakes, are similar to a Dutch Pancake. Now that I've confused things, here's a translation: To me, German Pancakes are made with fruit baked right into them, whereas the Dutch Pancake has fruit added after it's baked. Apples are the traditional fruit to use in this recipe, along with cinnamon and sugar, of course. Cottage cheese adds a tangy taste.

¼ cup all-purpose flour

1 tablespoon granulated sugar

¼ teaspoon baking powder

2 large eggs

¼ cup 2% milk

¼ cup small curd cottage cheese

2 tablespoons vegetable oil

2 tablespoons butter

2 tablespoons brown sugar

1 Granny Smith apple, peeled, cored, and sliced ⅛ inch thick

½ teaspoon cinnamon

1 In a medium bowl, combine the flour, sugar, and baking powder.

2 In a 2-cup glass measuring cup, whisk together the eggs, milk, cottage cheese, and oil until blended.

3 Pour the egg mixture into the flour mixture and stir just until combined. Let stand while you prepare the apple mixture.

4 Set or preheat the air fryer to 375°F. Put the butter in a 6-by-2-inch round pan and place the pan in the air fryer basket; cook for 1 minute and remove.

5 Swirl the pan so the butter coats the bottom and ½ inch up the sides. Top evenly with the brown sugar and apples, and sprinkle with the cinnamon.

6 Bake this mixture for 3 minutes or until the butter bubbles. Remove the pan.

7 Pour the batter over the apples. Return the pan to the air fryer and bake for 9 to 11 minutes or until the batter is golden brown. Cut into three wedges to serve.

SUBSTITUTION TIP: You could substitute sliced bananas for the apples for a Banana Pancake. Or even use ½ cup canned pineapple tidbits, drained, for a tropical spin.

Mushroom Scrambled Eggs

30 MINUTES, FAMILY-FRIENDLY, GLUTEN-FREE / SERVES 3

PREP TIME:
10 minutes

COOK TIME:
16 minutes

BAKE:
350°F

PER SERVING:
Calories: 246;
Protein: 14g;
Fat: 21g;
Saturated Fat: 10g;
Carbohydrates: 2g;
Sugar: 1g;
Sodium: 512g;
Fiber: 0g

INGREDIENT TIP:
You can make this recipe with olive oil instead of butter and use 3 whole eggs and 4 egg whites for a lower fat content. The recipe will still be delicious and flavorful.

Scrambled eggs are a cinch to make in the air fryer. They cook quickly at relatively low heat and are always tender and creamy. Mushrooms and some scallions are cooked first, then the eggs are stirred in and cooked until everything is done. Serve with gluten-free whole-grain toast and some orange juice for a great breakfast.

2 tablespoons butter

⅔ cup sliced mushrooms

1 scallion, chopped

6 large eggs

2 tablespoons light cream

½ teaspoon dried thyme

½ teaspoon sea salt

⅛ teaspoon freshly ground black pepper

1 Set or preheat the air fryer to 350°F.

2 Place the butter in a 6-by-2-inch round pan and put the pan in the air fryer basket and the basket in the fryer. Melt the butter in the air fryer for 1 minute.

3 Remove the basket and pan and add the mushrooms and scallions to the pan.

4 Return the basket to the air fryer and bake for 5 minutes or until the mushrooms are lightly browned, shaking the pan after 3 minutes.

5 Meanwhile, in a medium bowl, whisk together the eggs, light cream, thyme, salt, and pepper until combined.

6 Remove the air fryer basket and pour the egg mixture into the pan.

7 Return to the air fryer and bake for 8 to 10 minutes, stirring the egg mixture gently after 5 minutes, until the eggs are set. Serve.

Monkey Bread

30 MINUTES, FAMILY-FRIENDLY / SERVES 4

PREP TIME:
15 minutes

COOK TIME:
10 minutes

BAKE:
350°F

PER SERVING:
Calories: 369;
Protein: 5g;
Fat: 19g;
Saturated Fat: 11g;
Carbohydrates:
47g;
Sugar: 16g;
Sodium: 250g;
Fiber: 2g

Yes, you can make Monkey Bread in an air fryer! Balls coated in cinnamon sugar are baked into a delicious gooey and warm coffee cake. To serve, plate it whole and let everyone pull off their own sections from the bread.

Nonstick baking spray containing flour

1 cup all-purpose flour

¼ cup whole-wheat flour

1 tablespoon brown sugar

1 teaspoon baking powder

¼ teaspoon sea salt

6 tablespoons unsalted butter, melted, divided

5 tablespoons whole milk

¼ cup granulated sugar

1½ teaspoons cinnamon

1 Spray a 6-by-3-inch round pan with the baking spray and set aside.

2 In a small bowl, combine the all-purpose flour, whole-wheat flour, brown sugar, baking powder, and salt.

3 Stir in 3 tablespoons of melted butter and the milk and mix until a dough forms.

4 Divide the dough into 16 balls.

5 Combine the granulated sugar and cinnamon on a plate. Place the remaining 3 tablespoons of melted butter in a shallow bowl.

6 Dip the dough balls into the butter, then roll them in the cinnamon-sugar mixture to coat. As you work, drop the sugared dough balls into the prepared pan. Make sure the dough balls touch one another.

7 Set or preheat the air fryer to 350°F. Place the pan in the air fryer basket and the basket in the air fryer. Bake for 6 to 10 minutes or until the bread is deep golden brown.

8 Let cool on a rack for 3 minutes, then turn the pan over to remove the bread. Enjoy!

Nut and Berry Granola

30 MINUTES, FAMILY-FRIENDLY, GLUTEN-FREE / SERVES 6

PREP TIME:
15 minutes

COOK TIME:
12 minutes

BAKE:
350°F

PER SERVING:
Calories: 361;
Protein: 6g;
Fat: 21g;
Saturated Fat: 2g;
Carbohydrates:
38g;
Sugar: 18g;
Sodium: 82g;
Fiber: 5g

INGREDIENT TIP:
Make sure the oatmeal you buy is marked gluten-free. Some oats are processed on the same lines that also process wheat for flour and may contain traces of gluten.

Granola makes an excellent breakfast as well as a hearty snack. This recipe is full of nuts and dried blueberries and cherries. Serve it with some cold plant-based milk, such as soy or almond milk, for a great start to your day.

1½ cups rolled oats (not quick-cooking oats)

1 cup chopped pecans or walnuts, or a combination

3 tablespoons flaxseed

½ teaspoon cinnamon

⅛ teaspoon nutmeg

¼ cup maple syrup

3 tablespoons vegetable oil

1 teaspoon vanilla

¼ teaspoon sea salt

½ cup dried blueberries

½ cup dried cherries

1 In a large bowl, combine the oats, nuts, flaxseed, cinnamon, and nutmeg and mix well.

2 In a 2-cup glass measuring cup, combine the maple syrup, oil, vanilla, and salt and mix well. Pour this over the oat mixture and stir to combine.

3 Spread the mixture in a 7-inch round pan.

4 Set or preheat the air fryer to 350°F. Place the pan in the air fryer basket and the basket in the air fryer. Bake for 12 minutes, stirring halfway through cooking time, until the granola is golden brown and fragrant.

5 Transfer the granola to a serving bowl and let cool for 3 minutes. Stir in the dried blueberries and cherries. Let stand until cool, then serve, or store in an airtight container at room temperature for up to 4 days.

Banana Cranberry Bread

FAMILY-FRIENDLY / SERVES 4

PREP TIME:
15 minutes

COOK TIME:
33 minutes

BAKE:
325°F

PER SERVING:
Calories: 351;
Protein: 5g;
Fat: 13g;
Saturated Fat: 8g;
Carbohydrates:
55g;
Sugar: 33g;
Sodium: 315g;
Fiber: 2g

Banana bread made in the air fryer has a wonderfully moist crumb (the interior) and slightly crisp crust. Using a 6-inch round pan, you can serve moist and tender bread to four people in less than an hour. The air fryer works as a convection oven in this recipe, making a dense bread with delicious flavor.

Nonstick baking spray containing flour

¼ cup butter, at room temperature

¼ cup granulated sugar

¼ cup brown sugar

1 large ripe banana, mashed (about ⅔ cup)

1 large egg

¾ cup all-purpose flour

½ teaspoon cinnamon

¼ teaspoon sea salt

¼ teaspoon baking soda

⅛ teaspoon nutmeg

¼ cup buttermilk, divided

¼ cup dried cranberries

1 Spray a 6-inch round pan with the baking spray and set aside.

2 In a medium bowl, beat the butter with the granulated and brown sugars until smooth. Beat in the banana and egg until combined.

3 Combine the flour, cinnamon, salt, baking soda, and nutmeg in a small bowl and whisk well.

4 Stir one-third of the flour mixture into the banana mixture, then stir in half of the buttermilk. Stir in another third of the flour mixture, then the remaining buttermilk. Finally, add the remaining flour mixture, stirring just until combined. Stir in the cranberries just until evenly distributed.

5 Spoon the batter into the prepared pan.

6 Set or preheat the air fryer to 325°F. Put the pan in the air fryer basket and the basket in the air fryer. Bake for 28 to 33 minutes or until the bread is golden brown and springs back lightly when touched.

7 Cool on a wire rack, then cut into four wedges to serve.

AIR FRYER TIP: There must be 1 inch of space between the sides of the pan and the air fryer basket so the air can circulate around the bread as it bakes. Most air fryers will accommodate a 6-inch round pan.

Cheesy Corn Bread

FAMILY-FRIENDLY / SERVES 4

PREP TIME:
15 minutes

COOK TIME:
22 minutes

BAKE:
350°F

PER SERVING:
Calories: 367;
Protein: 12g;
Fat: 20g;
Saturated Fat: 12g;
Carbohydrates:
36g;
Sugar: 8g;
Sodium: 553g;
Fiber: 2g

Corn bread is a wonderful treat to serve alongside soups and stews, but it also makes a great breakfast. Eat it warm from the air fryer, or warm it up in the microwave and top with butter or honey.

Nonstick baking spray containing flour

⅔ cup yellow cornmeal

½ cup all-purpose flour

1 teaspoon baking powder

½ teaspoon baking soda

¼ teaspoon sea salt

½ cup shredded Cheddar cheese

1 cup buttermilk

2 large eggs

¼ cup butter, melted

1 tablespoon honey

1 Spray a 6-inch round pan with the baking spray and set aside.

2 Combine the cornmeal, flour, baking powder, baking soda, and salt in a medium bowl. Add the cheese and toss to coat.

3 In a glass measuring cup, combine the buttermilk, eggs, butter, and honey until smooth. Add this to the flour mixture and stir just until combined.

4 Spread the batter into the prepared pan.

5 Set or preheat the air fryer to 350°F. Put the pan in the air fryer basket and bake for 17 to 22 minutes or until the corn bread is golden brown and a toothpick inserted in the center comes out clean. Let cool on a wire rack for 15 minutes before cutting into four wedges to serve.

COOKING TIP: All quick breads (those made without yeast) should be mixed just until the dry ingredients and wet ingredients are combined. Stirring too much will develop the gluten in the flour and the bread will be tough.

Crustless Mini Quiches

FAMILY-FRIENDLY, GLUTEN-FREE / SERVES 3

PREP TIME:
20 minutes

COOK TIME:
15 minutes

BAKE:
325°F

PER SERVING:
Calories: 382;
Protein: 23g;
Fat: 27g;
Saturated Fat: 13g;
Carbohydrates: 11g;
Sugar: 1g;
Sodium: 400g;
Fiber: 1g

These muffin-size quiches are great for breakfast on the run. They are savory and hearty and full of wonderful flavor. They are easy to reheat, too: Just microwave each little quiche for 20 to 30 seconds until hot. Or reheat them in the air fryer for about 1 minute at 325°F.

6 large eggs

¼ cup sour cream

1 tablespoon cornstarch

½ cup frozen shredded hash brown potatoes, thawed

½ cup shredded Swiss cheese

½ cup shredded Colby cheese

1 scallion, chopped

1 tablespoon minced fresh chives

1 Place 6 silicone muffin cups in the air fryer basket and set aside.

2 In a large bowl, beat the eggs until scrambled. Add the sour cream and cornstarch and stir well.

3 Add the potatoes, Swiss and Colby cheeses, scallion, and chives and mix well.

4 Using a ¼-cup measure, divide the mixture among the muffin cups in the air fryer basket.

5 Set or preheat the air fryer to 325°F. Place the basket in the air fryer and bake for 15 minutes or until the quiches are puffed and light golden brown. Serve.

Sweet Potato Veggie Hash

FAMILY-FRIENDLY, GLUTEN-FREE / SERVES 4

PREP TIME:
15 minutes

COOK TIME:
28 minutes

BAKE:
400°F

_____

PER SERVING:
Calories: 176;
Protein: 4g;
Fat: 4g;
Saturated Fat: 1g;
Carbohydrates:
34g;
Sugar: 5g;
Sodium: 259g;
Fiber: 4g

_____

VARIATION TIP:
If you eat eggs,
fry up four
eggs and serve
them on top
of this hash.
You could
also sprinkle
some cheese
over the hash
after it's done
cooking so it
melts into the
potatoes. Cook
the eggs until
the yolks are
firm for food
safety reasons.

Hash used to be made up of leftovers, as a way for frugal people to eke another meal out of food already on hand. But hash is wonderful as a brand-new dish, too, and can be made with just about any vegetable you'd like. This tender and flavorful hash is great for a weekend brunch.

1 tablespoon olive oil

3 Yukon Gold potatoes, peeled and chopped

1 sweet potato, peeled and chopped

1 yellow onion, diced

1 red bell pepper, diced

2 garlic cloves, sliced

1 teaspoon dried thyme

½ teaspoon sea salt

⅛ teaspoon freshly ground black pepper

1 In a medium bowl, toss the olive oil with the Yukon Gold and sweet potatoes. Place in the air fryer basket.

2 Set or preheat the air fryer to 400°F. Place the basket in the air fryer and cook the potatoes for 15 minutes, stirring every 5 minutes, until they are tender.

3 Add the onion, bell pepper, garlic, thyme, salt, and pepper to the basket and toss with the potatoes.

4 Bake for 8 to 13 minutes longer, stirring halfway through cooking time, until the potatoes are browned and crisp and the vegetables are crisp-tender. Serve.

Spinach-Stuffed French Toast

30 MINUTES, FAMILY-FRIENDLY / SERVES 4

PREP TIME:
15 minutes

COOK TIME:
8 minutes

BAKE:
350°F

PER SERVING:
Calories: 378;
Protein: 18g;
Fat: 13g;
Saturated Fat: 7g;
Carbohydrates:
49g;
Sugar: 4g;
Sodium: 792g;
Fiber: 3g

French toast doesn't have to be sweet! This savory and hearty recipe is great for breakfast on a cold winter day. The cheesy spinach filling is a delicious twist on the classic sweet version. You can serve it with some warmed tomato sauce if you'd like.

½ cup shredded
Havarti cheese

½ cup frozen spinach,
thawed and well-drained

4 tablespoons (2 ounces)
cream cheese, at
room temperature

2 scallions, chopped

1 garlic clove, minced

½ teaspoon dried marjoram

¼ teaspoon sea salt

⅛ teaspoon freshly
ground black pepper

4 (1¼-inch-thick) slices
French bread

2 large eggs

¼ cup whole milk

½ cup dried bread crumbs

1 In a medium bowl, combine the Havarti, spinach, cream cheese, scallions, garlic, marjoram, salt, and pepper and mix well.

2 Cut a slit in the side of each piece of French bread about 2 inches wide. Do not go through to the other side; you are creating a pocket.

3 Stuff the pockets with the spinach mixture. Press the slices gently to close.

4 In a shallow bowl, beat the eggs with the milk until smooth. Place the French bread slices into the egg mixture, turning once, letting the bread absorb most of the egg mixture.

5 Place the bread crumbs on a plate. Dip the egg-soaked bread slices into the bread crumbs; pat down on them so they adhere to the slices.

6 Set or preheat the air fryer to 350°F. Put the bread slices in the air fryer basket and the basket in the air fryer. Cook for 3 to 4 minutes on each side, turning once, until the bread is browned and crisp. Serve.

INGREDIENT TIP: Frozen spinach really needs to be drained well for this recipe. Squeeze out as much liquid as you can, then put the spinach between some paper towels and press down to squeeze out more moisture.

*Crispy Buffalo
Cauliflower Bites*
PAGE 49

SNACKS
& BITES

Cheese-Filled Bread Bowl

FAMILY-FRIENDLY / SERVES 6

PREP TIME:
10 minutes

COOK TIME:
28 minutes

BAKE:
375°F

———————

PER SERVING:
Calories: 514;
Protein: 17g;
Fat: 42g;
Saturated Fat: 18g;
Carbohydrates: 17g;
Sugar: 1g;
Sodium: 743g;
Fiber: 1g

This comforting and unexpected appetizer is made from a hollowed-out loaf of bread, filled with a creamy cheese dip. It's simple to make and everyone loves it. You can also serve this with carrot and celery sticks, strips of yellow and red bell peppers, or any other raw veggies for dipping.

1 (6-inch) round loaf bread, unsliced

2 tablespoons olive oil

6 ounces cream cheese, at room temperature

½ cup mayonnaise

¼ cup whole milk

1 cup shredded Havarti cheese

1 cup shredded provolone cheese

¼ cup grated Parmesan cheese

2 scallions, sliced

1 teaspoon Worcestershire sauce

1 Cut the top 1 inch of the bread off. Use a serrated bread knife to cut around the inside of the loaf, leaving about a 1-inch shell. Be careful not to cut through the bottom. Cut the pieces of bread and the top of the loaf into 1-inch cubes and drizzle with the olive oil.

2 Set or preheat the air fryer to 375°F. Put the bread cubes in the air fryer basket and bake for 5 to 8 minutes, shaking halfway through cooking time, until toasted. Place in a serving bowl. Keep the air fryer set to 375°F.

3 Meanwhile, beat the cream cheese with the mayonnaise and milk until smooth. Stir in the Havarti, provolone, and Parmesan cheeses, scallions, and Worcestershire sauce.

4 Spoon the cheese mixture into the center of the bread shell. Put the filled bread in the air fryer basket and place the basket in the air fryer.

5 Bake at 375°F for 15 to 20 minutes, stirring the mixture halfway through cooking time, until the cheese is melted and starts to brown on top. Serve with the toasted bread and bread sticks, if desired.

INGREDIENT TIP: Make sure the bread fits into the air fryer basket with about an inch of space all the way around so it will bake evenly.

Apricots in Blankets

5 INGREDIENTS, FAMILY-FRIENDLY / SERVES 6

PREP TIME:
20 minutes

COOK TIME:
24 minutes

BAKE:
375°F

PER SERVING:
Calories: 137;
Protein: 2g;
Fat: 9g;
Saturated Fat: 5g;
Carbohydrates: 12g;
Sugar: 5g;
Sodium: 117g;
Fiber: 1g

COOKING TIP:
You can make these little pastries in advance, cool for 30 minutes, then refrigerate. Reheat right in the air fryer for 4 to 5 minutes at 375°F, until they are hot.

Everyone has heard of Figs in Blankets, where dried figs are stuffed with cheese, wrapped in dough and baked. Using dried apricots instead of figs is a nice twist on the classic recipe and offers a different taste, especially with a little tang from the honey mustard. Thaw the puff pastry in the refrigerator the night before you want to make these delectable treats.

6 dried apricots,
halved lengthwise

4 tablespoons (2 ounces)
cream cheese

½ sheet frozen puff
pastry, thawed

4 tablespoons
honey mustard

2 tablespoons
butter, melted

1 Stuff each apricot half with a teaspoon of cream cheese and set aside.

2 Roll out the puff pastry until it is 6 by 12 inches. Cut in half lengthwise for two 3-by-12-inch rectangles. Cut each rectangle into six 3-inch strips for a total of 12 puff pastry strips.

3 Spread 1 teaspoon of honey mustard onto each strip. Place a filled apricot on each strip and roll up the pastry, pinching the seam closed but leaving the ends open.

4 Place 6 filled pastries in the air fryer basket. Brush the top of each with some of the melted butter.

5 Set or preheat the air fryer to 375°F. Put the basket in the air fryer. Bake for 8 to 12 minutes or until the pastry is golden brown. Repeat with the other six pastries, then serve.

Fried Ravioli with Blue Cheese Dipping Sauce

30 MINUTES, FAMILY-FRIENDLY / SERVES 4 TO 6

PREP TIME:
15 minutes

COOK TIME:
13 minutes

FRY:
400°F

PER SERVING:
Calories: 456;
Protein: 20g;
Fat: 21g;
Saturated Fat: 12g;
Carbohydrates: 46g;
Sugar: 4g;
Sodium: 633g;
Fiber: 2g

Fried ravioli are a fabulous snack that takes just minutes to prepare. Frozen ravioli are coated in egg, bread crumbs, and seasonings, and air fried until they are tender and crisp. The dipping sauce is super simple to make, too. Offer this snack at your next football party.

⅔ cup sour cream

⅓ cup crumbled blue cheese

3 tablespoons whole milk

1 large egg, beaten

1 tablespoon water

1 teaspoon dried Italian seasoning

1 cup dried bread crumbs

⅓ cup grated Parmesan cheese

½ (25-ounce) bag frozen cheese ravioli

Olive oil spray

1 In a small serving bowl, combine the sour cream, blue cheese, and milk and stir to combine. Cover and refrigerate while you prepare the ravioli.

2 In a shallow bowl, whisk together the egg, water, and Italian seasoning until combined. On a plate, combine the bread crumbs and Parmesan cheese and mix.

3 Dip the frozen ravioli, two at a time, into the egg, then into the bread crumb mixture pressing gently to adhere the coating. Put the coated ravioli in the air fryer basket as you work. Spray every layer with some olive oil.

4 When all of the ravioli are coated, in the basket, and sprayed with oil, set or preheat the air fryer to 400°F. Fry for 10 to 13 minutes, shaking the basket halfway through, until the ravioli are hot and crisp on the outside.

5 Serve the ravioli with the dipping sauce.

Roasted Baby Veggies with Dip

FAMILY-FRIENDLY, GLUTEN-FREE / SERVES 6

PREP TIME:
15 minutes

COOK TIME:
21 minutes

ROAST:
400°F

PER SERVING:
Calories: 161;
Protein: 3g;
Fat: 10g;
Saturated Fat: 4g;
Carbohydrates: 16g;
Sugar: 4g;
Sodium: 419g;
Fiber: 3g

SUBSTITUTION TIP: You can roast tender vegetables such as sliced bell peppers, broccoli florets, green beans, and cauliflower using this same method. The cooking times will reduce to 5 minutes, then 5 minutes, then 3 minutes.

Roasted baby vegetables, when cooked with olive oil and herbs, make a wonderful snack or appetizer. These little root veggies become so sweet and tender when they are roasted; even kids will like them! Serve them with little toothpicks to encourage dipping into the sour cream dip.

2 cups baby potatoes

1½ cups baby carrots

1½ cups baby beets, peeled

12 garlic cloves, peeled

2 tablespoons olive oil, divided

1 teaspoon sea salt

⅛ teaspoon freshly ground black pepper

½ cup sour cream

3 tablespoons crumbled blue or feta cheese

1½ teaspoons dried thyme, divided

1 teaspoon dried marjoram

1 Put the potatoes, carrots, beets, and garlic cloves in the air fryer basket. Drizzle with 1 tablespoon of olive oil and sprinkle with the salt and pepper. Toss to coat.

2 Set or preheat the air fryer to 400°F. Put the basket in the air fryer. Roast for 8 minutes.

3 Meanwhile, in a small bowl, combine the sour cream, cheese, and ½ teaspoon of thyme; mix and set aside.

4 Remove the basket and toss the vegetables. Put the basket back into the air fryer and continue roasting for another 8 minutes until the vegetables are almost tender. Drizzle with the remaining 1 tablespoon of oil and sprinkle with the marjoram and remaining 1 teaspoon of thyme; toss gently to coat.

5 Roast for 3 to 5 minutes more, or until the vegetables are tender. Serve with the dipping sauce.

Crispy Buffalo Cauliflower Bites

5 INGREDIENTS, 30 MINUTES, GLUTEN-FREE / SERVES 6

PREP TIME:
10 minutes

COOK TIME:
15 minutes
per batch

ROAST:
375°F

_____

PER SERVING:
Calories: 116;
Protein: 4g;
Fat: 5g;
Saturated Fat: 3g;
Carbohydrates: 17g;
Sugar: 7g;
Sodium: 326g;
Fiber: 4g

_____

**SUBSTITUTION
TIP:** You can
make this
recipe with
broccoli florets
as well—just
reduce the
cooking time
to about
10 minutes per
batch. Roasted
broccoli is
delicious
when cooked
until tender
and crisp in
this recipe.

Air-fried Buffalo cauliflower is even better than traditional Buffalo wings! The little florets are coated in hot sauce, then rolled in bread crumbs and roasted until they are crisp on the outside and tender on the inside. This type of recipe is traditionally served with celery sticks and blue cheese dressing, which provide cooling contrast.

1 large head cauliflower, broken into florets

3 tablespoons hot sauce

2 tablespoons butter, melted

1 tablespoon honey

½ cup dried bread crumbs

Cooking oil spray

1 In a large bowl, combine the cauliflower, hot sauce, butter, and honey and toss to coat the florets.

2 Sprinkle the cauliflower with the bread crumbs and toss to coat.

3 Working in two or three batches, place the florets in a single layer in the air fryer basket. Spritz with some cooking oil spray.

4 Set or preheat the air fryer to 375°F and roast 12 to 15 minutes, shaking the basket once during cooking time, until the cauliflower is crisp. Remove the cauliflower from the basket and put on a baking sheet in a 250°F oven to keep warm. Repeat with remaining cauliflower.

5 Serve warm with more hot sauce, blue cheese salad dressing, and celery sticks, if desired.

Tandoori-Style Chickpeas

5 INGREDIENTS, 30 MINUTES, GLUTEN-FREE / SERVES 6

PREP TIME:
5 minutes

COOK TIME:
15 minutes

ROAST:
400°F

PER SERVING:
Calories: 72;
Protein: 4g;
Fat: 1g;
Saturated Fat: 0g;
Carbohydrates: 12g;
Sugar: 2g;
Sodium: 4g;
Fiber: 4g

Chickpeas, or garbanzo beans, are little legumes that become crisp and tender when roasted in the air fryer. The seasoning for this recipe is Indian-inspired. A tandoor is actually a type of clay oven used to bake bread and meats. This spicy little appetizer is great to take along for snacks, whether you're having a picnic or going to watch the big game.

1 (15-ounce) can chickpeas, drained and rinsed

Cooking oil spray

2 teaspoons curry powder

1 teaspoon smoked paprika

1 teaspoon ground cumin

½ teaspoon cayenne pepper

1 Pat the chickpeas dry with paper towels and put in the air fryer basket.

2 Set or preheat the air fryer to 400°F. Place the basket in the air fryer and roast the chickpeas for 5 minutes.

3 Remove the basket and spray the chickpeas with some cooking oil; toss.

4 Return the basket to the air fryer and roast for 8 minutes more, shaking the basket once during cooking time.

5 Meanwhile, in a small bowl combine the curry powder, paprika, cumin, and cayenne pepper.

6 Remove the basket from the air fryer and sprinkle with the spice mixture; toss to coat. Continue roasting for 2 minutes or until the chickpeas are fragrant.

7 Let the chickpeas cool for about 10 minutes, then serve.

Roasted Garlic and Onion Dip

FAMILY-FRIENDLY, GLUTEN-FREE / SERVES 6

PREP TIME:
10 minutes

COOK TIME:
30 minutes

ROAST:
400°F

PER SERVING:
Calories: 299;
Protein: 3g;
Fat: 31g;
Saturated Fat: 12g;
Carbohydrates: 3g;
Sugar: 0g;
Sodium: 314g;
Fiber: 0g

COOKING TIP:
Feel free to roast the garlic in advance. You can mash the garlic and combine it with the cream cheese mixture when you're ready to serve the dip.

When roasted in its own skin, garlic becomes very tender, sweet, and nutty tasting, completely unlike the unroasted version. Some fresh scallions and minced chives are added to this recipe to add more of a sharp onion taste. Serve with crudités, crackers, chips, or breadsticks.

2 heads garlic

1 tablespoon olive oil

1 (8-ounce) package cream cheese, at room temperature

½ cup mayonnaise

2 tablespoons heavy (whipping) cream

¼ teaspoon sea salt

3 scallions, sliced

1 tablespoon minced fresh chives

1 Using a very sharp knife, cut off and discard the top 1 inch of the garlic heads, exposing the cloves. Drizzle each head with the olive oil.

2 Loosely wrap the garlic heads in aluminum foil and place in the air fryer basket.

3 Set or preheat the air fryer to 400°F. Put the basket in the air fryer and roast the garlic for 20 to 30 minutes, opening one foil packet after 20 minutes to see if the garlic cloves are soft. Continue roasting if needed.

4 Remove the foil packets from the air fryer, unwrap the garlic heads, and let cool on a wire rack for 20 minutes.

5 Separate the garlic cloves from the head and remove the papery skins; place the cloves in a medium bowl. Mash together until smooth.

6 Beat the cream cheese with the mayonnaise, heavy cream, and salt until smooth. Beat in the roasted garlic paste until well mixed, then stir in the scallions and chives. Serve.

Parmesan Avocado Fries with Guacamole

30 MINUTES, FAMILY-FRIENDLY / SERVES 4

PREP TIME:
15 minutes

COOK TIME:
6 minutes per batch

FRY:
400°F

───────────

PER SERVING:
Calories: 463;
Protein: 12g;
Fat: 35g;
Saturated Fat: 8g;
Carbohydrates: 31g;
Sugar: 2g;
Sodium: 444g;
Fiber: 13g

If one form of avocado is good in a recipe, two is even better! These crisp and soft little fries made of avocado slices are fabulous dipped into a cool and flavorful guacamole for double the avocado taste. You may want to make a double batch of these fries, since they will go fast!

- 4 ripe avocados, divided
- 2 tablespoons freshly squeezed lemon juice
- ⅓ cup sour cream
- ½ teaspoon sea salt
- ⅛ teaspoon freshly ground black pepper
- ⅓ cup all-purpose flour
- 1 large egg
- 2 tablespoons whole milk
- ⅓ cup panko bread crumbs
- 3 tablespoons grated Parmesan cheese

1 Remove the flesh from 2 avocados (see Tip); place in a bowl and sprinkle with the lemon juice.

2 Mash the avocados and stir in the sour cream, salt, and pepper. Cover with plastic wrap, gently pressing the plastic over the surface of the guacamole. This will keep it from browning. Refrigerate.

3 Halve the remaining 2 avocados and gently twist to separate the halves. Remove the pits by striking them with a chef's knife; twist to remove the pit. Cut each half lengthwise into 4 slices, removing the peel.

4 Put the flour on a plate. Put the egg and milk into a shallow bowl and beat to combine. Put the bread crumbs and Parmesan cheese on a plate and combine.

5 Dip the avocado slices into the flour. Shake off any excess flour, then dip each slice into the egg mixture. Place in the bread crumbs, then flip to coat both sides. Shake off any excess crumbs.

6 Set or preheat the air fryer to 400°F. Working in batches if needed, put the coated avocado slices in a single layer in the air fryer basket. Put the basket in the air fryer and fry for 6 minutes, turning the slices over halfway through cooking time, until the fries are crisp.

7 Serve the fries with the guacamole.

INGREDIENT TIP: The best way to remove avocado flesh from the rind is to halve the fruit lengthwise, remove the pit, then take a large spoon and run it between the flesh and the skin. That will remove the entire half without breaking it.

Southwest Egg Rolls

FAMILY-FRIENDLY / SERVES 10

PREP TIME:
20 minutes

COOK TIME:
15 minutes
per batch

FRY:
375°F

PER SERVING:
Calories: 376;
Protein: 17g;
Fat: 6g;
Saturated Fat: 3g;
Carbohydrates:
68g;
Sugar: 3g;
Sodium: 675g;
Fiber: 5g

AIR FRYER TIP:
The number of
egg rolls you
can cook at
one time will
depend on the
size of your
air fryer. Don't
crowd food in
the basket; air
circulation is
needed around
each piece
so the food
cooks and
crisps evenly.
You can keep
the cooked
food warm in
a 250°F oven
until you are
ready to serve.

Egg rolls are the quintessential appetizer, but they don't have to be made with Asian ingredients. Try serving these with guacamole to cool down the kick from the pepper. If spicy is not to everyone's tastes, skip the jalapeño.

1 cup frozen corn
kernels, thawed

1 (15-ounce) can pinto
beans, drained and rinsed

½ cup chopped plum
tomatoes, drained

2 scallions, chopped

1 jalapeño pepper, minced

1½ cups shredded
pepper Jack cheese

2 teaspoons chili powder

½ teaspoon dried oregano

¼ teaspoon garlic powder

1 (20-count) package
egg roll wrappers

Cooking oil spray

1 In a large bowl, combine the corn, pinto beans, tomatoes, scallions, and jalapeño pepper until well mixed.

2 Add the cheese, chili powder, oregano, and garlic powder and mix well.

3 Place an egg roll wrapper on a work surface. Brush the edges with a bit of water, then place a heaping 2 tablespoons of the corn mixture in the middle. Fold one edge of the egg roll wrapper over the filling, fold in the sides, and roll up. Press the seam to secure. Repeat with the remaining filling and egg roll wrappers.

4 Set or preheat the air fryer to 375°F. Working in batches, put the egg rolls in the basket in a single layer, making sure they don't touch each other. Spray with cooking oil.

5 Place the basket in the air fryer and fry for 10 minutes. Remove the basket and turn the egg rolls over; spray them once more with oil. Return the basket and fry for another 5 minutes or until crisp. Repeat with remaining egg rolls. Let cool for 10 minutes, then serve.

Jalapeño Poppers

SERVES 6

PREP TIME:
15 minutes

COOK TIME:
12 minutes
per batch

FRY:
400°F

_____

PER SERVING:
Calories: 238;
Protein: 9g;
Fat: 20g;
Saturated Fat: 10g;
Carbohydrates: 6g;
Sugar: 1g;
Sodium: 266g;
Fiber: 1g

_____

INGREDIENT TIP:
If you like
really hot
peppers, don't
remove the
seeds and
membranes
from the
jalapeños. The
seeds and
membranes
contain most
of the cap-
saicin, the
chemical that
causes the
hot taste.

Jalapeño poppers are a perennial sports bar snack. The little hot chiles are stuffed with a cheesy mixture, then fried to golden brown goodness. Some menus go all out and wrap them in bacon to contain the cheese. In this recipe the jalapeños are wrapped in flaky dough to create a delectable bite.

12 jalapeño peppers

4 ounces cream cheese, at room temperature

2 tablespoons mayonnaise

1 cup shredded Cheddar cheese

¼ cup grated Parmesan cheese

All-purpose flour, for dusting

1 sheet frozen puff pastry, thawed

1 Halve the jalapeño peppers lengthwise, cut off the stem, and remove the membranes and seeds. Set aside.

2 In a medium bowl, combine the cream cheese and mayonnaise and beat until smooth. Mix in the Cheddar and Parmesan cheeses. Fill 12 of the jalapeño pepper halves with equal parts of this mixture, then top them with the other pepper half to make 12 poppers.

3 Dust a clean work surface with some flour. Roll out the puff pastry into a 12-inch square. Cut the square in half, then cut each half into twelve 1-by-6-inch rectangular strips.

4 Wind a puff pastry strip around a filled jalapeño half in a spiral shape. Repeat for all the puff pastry strips and stuffed jalapeños.

5 Working in batches, put the filled and wrapped jalapeño peppers in the air fryer basket in a single layer; don't let them touch each other.

6 Set or preheat the air fryer to 400°F. Put the basket in the air fryer and fry for 10 to 12 minutes or until the pastry is golden brown. Repeat with remaining poppers.

Sweet Potato Tots

5 INGREDIENTS, FAMILY-FRIENDLY / SERVES 8

PREP TIME:
15 minutes

COOK TIME:
17 minutes
per batch

FRY:
400°F

_____

PER SERVING:
Calories: 109;
Protein: 4g;
Fat: 4g;
Saturated Fat: 1g;
Carbohydrates:
16g;
Sugar: 2g;
Sodium: 281g;
Fiber: 2g

_____

**SUBSTITUTION
TIP:** You can
make these
tots with spicy
ingredients
instead of
sweet if you'd
like. Omit
the nutmeg
and add
2 teaspoons
chili powder
and
¼ teaspoon
cayenne
pepper.

Tater tots are the classic recipe made of deep-fried shredded potatoes. This recipe uses sweet potatoes for a nice twist, and adds some cheese for texture and flavor. Just start with canned sweet potatoes, add a few more ingredients, and you'll get a flavorful tot that everyone will love.

1 (15-ounce) can sweet potatoes, drained

½ cup grated Parmesan cheese

1 large egg white

½ teaspoon sea salt

⅛ teaspoon nutmeg

1 cup crushed cracker crumbs, such as Ritz or club crackers

Cooking oil spray

1 Put the sweet potatoes in a medium bowl and mash them. Stir in the Parmesan cheese, egg white, salt, and nutmeg until well mixed.

2 Create the tots by forming 1 tablespoon of the sweet potato mixture into rounded rectangles.

3 Put the cracker crumbs on a plate. Roll each of the tots in the crumbs to coat.

4 Working in batches, put the tots in a single layer in the air fryer basket and spray with the cooking oil.

5 Set or preheat the air fryer to 400°F. Put the basket in the air fryer and fry for 14 to 17 minutes, turning once, until the tots are crisp and golden brown. Repeat with the remaining sweet potato mixture; serve hot.

Radish Chips

5 INGREDIENTS, GLUTEN-FREE / SERVES 8

PREP TIME:
20 minutes

COOK TIME:
18 minutes

FRY:
400°F

PER SERVING:
Calories: 17;
Protein: 0g;
Fat: 2g;
Saturated Fat: 0g;
Carbohydrates: 1g;
Sugar: 0g;
Sodium: 121g;
Fiber: 0g

We have all seen, and eaten, great recipes for kale chips, sweet potato chips, even parsnip chips and carrot chips. But what about radish chips? This fun recipe transforms sharp and spicy radishes into sweet and crispy little chips. The only difficult thing about this recipe is cutting the radishes into thin rounds. If you have a mandoline, definitely use it.

8 large radishes

1 tablespoon olive oil

½ teaspoon sea salt

1 teaspoon curry powder

1 Scrub the radishes and trim off the stem and root ends.

2 Using a sharp knife or mandoline, slice the radishes into thin rounds, about ⅛ inch thick. Pat the radish slices dry with a paper towel.

3 Put the radishes into the air fryer basket and drizzle with the oil; toss to coat. Sprinkle with the salt and toss again.

4 Set or preheat the air fryer to 400°F. Place the basket in the air fryer and fry for 14 to 18 minutes, tossing once during cooking time, until the radish chips are crisp and light golden brown. Remove the basket; sprinkle the chips with the curry powder and toss.

5 Serve immediately or let cool and store in an airtight container at room temperature for up to 3 days.

Spinach-Cranberry Turnovers

FAMILY-FRIENDLY / SERVES 6

PREP TIME:
20 minutes

COOK TIME:
12 minutes
per batch

BAKE:
375°F

_____

PER SERVING:
Calories: 189;
Protein: 3g;
Fat: 14g;
Saturated Fat: 8g;
Carbohydrates: 15g;
Sugar: 7g;
Sodium: 171g;
Fiber: 1g

_____

INGREDIENT TIP:
The size of the
phyllo sheets
can vary. When
you cut the
dough into
strips, make
sure the strips
are at least
3-inches wide
to hold the
filling. This
recipe makes
12 triangles.

Savory turnovers make great appetizers. You can fill these little triangles with all kinds of wonderful ingredients. This recipe combines spinach, which is slightly bitter, with tart and sweet cranberries and some cream cheese.

4 ounces cream cheese, at room temperature

2 tablespoons sour cream

1 cup frozen chopped spinach, thawed and drained

⅓ cup dried cranberries, chopped

3 (9-by-14-inch) sheets frozen phyllo dough, thawed

3 tablespoons butter, melted

1 In a medium bowl, beat the cream cheese and sour cream until blended. Stir in the spinach and cranberries until well mixed. Set aside.

2 Place the phyllo dough on the work surface and cover with a damp towel. Remove one sheet of phyllo and cut it into four 3½-by-9-inch rectangles.

3 Place a tablespoon of the filling at the bottom of one of the rectangles, with the short side facing you. Fold the phyllo into triangles (like you would fold a flag), then brush with butter to seal the edges. Repeat with remaining phyllo, filling, and butter.

4 Set or preheat the air fryer to 375°F. Put 4 to 6 triangles in the air fryer basket in a single layer. Put the basket in the air fryer and bake for 11 to 12 minutes or until the triangles are golden brown, turning over halfway through cooking time. Repeat with the remaining turnovers. Serve.

Mushroom Toast with Ginger and Sesame

FAMILY-FRIENDLY / SERVES 6

PREP TIME:
20 minutes

COOK TIME:
**8 minutes
per batch**

FRY:
375°F

———————

PER SERVING:
Calories: 80;
Protein: 4g;
Fat: 4g;
Saturated Fat: 1g;
Carbohydrates: 9g;
Sugar: 2g;
Sodium: 221g;
Fiber: 2g

———————

INGREDIENT TIP:
Canned mushrooms are used to save time; it can take up to 30 minutes to sauté fresh mushrooms. If you want to use fresh mushrooms, bake them by themselves in the air fryer for 15 to 20 minutes until they give up their liquid and turn brown.

Mushroom toast is a vegetarian version of shrimp toast, that popular appetizer offered on many Asian menus. Instead of shrimp, mushrooms are ground to a paste and seasoned with fresh ginger, soy sauce, and scallions. The mixture is spread on bread, topped with sesame seeds, and then "fried" in the air fryer until crisp and brown.

2 teaspoons olive oil

2 (4-ounce) cans sliced mushrooms, drained

3 scallions, sliced

1 tablespoon grated fresh ginger

1 tablespoon soy sauce

3 slices whole-wheat bread

2 tablespoons sesame seeds

1 Heat the olive oil in a medium saucepan over medium heat. Add the mushrooms and cook, stirring often, for 3 to 4 minutes or until the mushrooms are dry.

2 Add the scallions, ginger, and soy sauce and cook for another 3 minutes or until the mushrooms have absorbed the soy sauce.

3 Transfer the mixture to a blender or food processor and process until it forms a paste.

4 Cut the bread slices into fourths, making triangles. Spread the mushroom mixture onto the bread triangles, dividing evenly, then sprinkle with the sesame seeds.

5 Set or preheat the air fryer to 375°F. Working in batches, place the triangles in the air fryer basket in a single layer. Fry for 7 to 8 minutes or until the toast is crisp. Repeat with the remaining triangles. Serve.

Grape Focaccia Bites

5 INGREDIENTS, FAMILY-FRIENDLY / SERVES 4

PREP TIME:
15 minutes

COOK TIME:
28 minutes

BAKE:
350°F

PER SERVING:
Calories: 259;
Protein: 4g;
Fat: 15g;
Saturated Fat: 2g;
Carbohydrates:
28g;
Sugar: 3g;
Sodium: 245g;
Fiber: 1g

Most focaccia bread is made with yeast; this version doesn't use yeast so the preparation time is much shorter. Red grapes are baked right into the dough; they provide a sweet burst of flavor when you bite into this tender bread.

1 cup all-purpose flour

½ teaspoon sea salt

1½ teaspoons baking powder

⅓ cup whole milk

4 tablespoons olive oil, divided

⅔ cup halved red grapes

2 teaspoons fresh thyme

1 In a medium bowl, combine the flour, salt, and baking powder and mix well.

2 Add the milk and 3 tablespoons of the olive oil and stir just until a dough forms. Divide the dough into two balls.

3 Cut two pieces of parchment paper to fit in your air fryer basket. Press the dough onto each piece of paper, spreading the dough so it almost fills the paper.

4 Press down with your fingers to dimple the dough. Drizzle both with the remaining 1 tablespoon olive oil.

5 Put the grapes on the dough, cut-side down, and press down gently. Sprinkle with the thyme. Place one of the parchment pieces with dough in the air fryer basket.

6 Set or preheat the air fryer to 350°F. Put the basket in the air fryer and bake for 11 to 14 minutes or until the bread is golden brown. Remove the focaccia and repeat with the remaining dough.

7 Cut into squares and serve.

Parmesan Asparagus
PAGE 65

CHAPTER FOUR

SIDES

Roasted Waldorf Salad

30 MINUTES, FAMILY-FRIENDLY, GLUTEN-FREE / SERVES 4

PREP TIME:
15 minutes

COOK TIME:
14 minutes

ROAST:
400°F

PER SERVING:
Calories: 408;
Protein: 2g;
Fat: 33g;
Saturated Fat: 4g;
Carbohydrates:
29g;
Sugar: 23g;
Sodium: 193g;
Fiber: 5g

VARIATION TIP:
You can also
toast the
pecans in the
air fryer for
maximum
crunch. Set
the air fryer
to 300°F and
place the nuts
in the basket.
Toast for about
5 minutes or
until the nuts
are fragrant.
Let cool before
you add them
to the salad.

The Waldorf is a classic salad first served at the Waldorf-Astoria Hotel in 1893. It's made of chopped apples, celery, grapes, and nuts in a creamy dressing. Roasting the apples and grapes intensifies their flavors and adds interesting texture to this wonderful salad. The celery and pecans add crunch.

2 Granny Smith apples, cored and cut into chunks

2 teaspoons olive oil, divided

1½ cups red grapes

½ cup mayonnaise

2 tablespoons freshly squeezed lemon juice

1 tablespoon honey

3 celery stalks, sliced

½ cup coarsely chopped pecans

1 Put the chopped apples in the air fryer basket and drizzle with 1 teaspoon olive oil; toss to coat.

2 Set or preheat the air fryer for 400°F. Place the basket in the air fryer and roast for 4 minutes. Remove the basket.

3 Add the grapes to the basket and drizzle with the remaining 1 teaspoon of olive oil; toss again. Return the basket to the air fryer and roast for 8 to 10 minutes longer, shaking the basket halfway through cooking time, until tender.

4 Meanwhile, whisk together the mayonnaise, lemon juice, and honey in a medium bowl.

5 Add the celery and pecans to the dressing and stir to combine.

6 Place the roasted apples and grapes in the bowl and stir gently to coat the fruit with the dressing. Serve or refrigerate for 2 hours before serving.

Parmesan Asparagus

5 INGREDIENTS, 30 MINUTES, FAMILY-FRIENDLY, GLUTEN-FREE / SERVES 4

PREP TIME:
5 minutes

COOK TIME:
8 minutes

ROAST:
400°F

―――――――

PER SERVING:
Calories: 87;
Protein: 6g;
Fat: 6g;
Saturated Fat: 2g;
Carbohydrates: 5g;
Sugar: 2g;
Sodium: 334g;
Fiber: 2g

―――――――

INGREDIENT TIP:
Asparagus can have sand lodged into its flower end, so make sure you rinse it thoroughly. Save the tough stem ends to make soup.

Fresh asparagus is one of the nicest things about spring. Sure, you can buy asparagus year-round, but the spears harvested in the spring are much more tender and flavorful. Roasted with some olive oil, this super simple side dish is great with any main dish.

1 pound fresh asparagus

1 tablespoon olive oil

1 teaspoon freshly squeezed lemon juice

½ teaspoon sea salt

⅛ teaspoon freshly ground black pepper

3 tablespoons grated Parmesan cheese

1. Rinse the asparagus and snap off the woody ends where they break naturally.

2. Put the asparagus in the air fryer basket and drizzle with the olive oil and lemon juice, then sprinkle with the salt and pepper; toss to coat. Sprinkle with the Parmesan cheese and toss again.

3. Set or preheat the air fryer to 400°F. Place the basket in the air fryer and roast for 7 to 8 minutes, shaking once during cooking time, until the asparagus are tender and the cheese is light golden brown in places. Serve.

Melting Baby Potatoes

5 INGREDIENTS, FAMILY-FRIENDLY, GLUTEN-FREE / SERVES 4

PREP TIME:
15 minutes

COOK TIME:
27 minutes

ROAST:
400°F

PER SERVING:
Calories: 235;
Protein: 5g;
Fat: 7g;
Saturated Fat: 2g;
Carbohydrates:
40g;
Sugar: 3g;
Sodium: 333g;
Fiber: 6g

Traditional melting potatoes are first browned in high heat, then simmered in vegetable broth until they are tender. The potatoes have crisp skins and velvety interiors. This recipe, using baby potatoes, is a two-stage process, so it takes a bit longer than other air-fried potato recipes, but the results are worth it.

10 to 12 baby Yukon
   Gold potatoes
1 tablespoon olive oil
1 tablespoon butter, melted
½ teaspoon sea salt

⅛ teaspoon freshly
   ground black pepper
½ teaspoon dried thyme
⅓ cup vegetable broth

1 Scrub the potatoes and then cut them in half.

2 Put the olive oil and butter in a 7-inch round pan and swirl to coat the bottom. Add the potatoes, cut side down, in a single layer. You may have to use more or fewer potatoes, depending on how many will fit in the pan. The cut side has to sit flat on the pan bottom.

3 Put the pan in the air fryer basket and place the basket in the air fryer. Set or preheat to 400°F and roast the potatoes for 12 minutes. Remove the pan from the basket and shake to loosen the potatoes.

4 Sprinkle the potatoes with the salt, pepper, and thyme and pour the vegetable broth into the pan around the potatoes.

5 Return to the air fryer and roast for another 10 to 15 minutes or until the liquid is absorbed and the potatoes are tender when pierced with a fork. Serve.

INGREDIENT TIP: Baby Yukon Gold potatoes are used in this recipe because they naturally taste and look buttery, but you could substitute other small potatoes if you'd like. Try creamer potatoes, baby red potatoes, or new potatoes, but only if they are a little more than 1 inch in diameter. You can use fingerling potatoes if you cut them into thirds; turn the ones with two cut sides over when you add the broth.

Roasted Spicy Corn

30 MINUTES, FAMILY-FRIENDLY, GLUTEN-FREE / SERVES 4

PREP TIME:
5 minutes

COOK TIME:
15 minutes

ROAST:
400°F

PER SERVING:
Calories: 180;
Protein: 3g;
Fat: 12g;
Saturated Fat: 7g;
Carbohydrates:
18g;
Sugar: 3g;
Sodium: 300g;
Fiber: 3g

I like corn cut off the cob. But for some reason it's difficult to find a recipe for air-roasted corn off the cob. So, I came up with my own. This recipe is so simple to make, and everyone will love it. Adjust the spice level to the amount your family likes. This creamy and savory recipe is delicious.

2 cups frozen corn kernels, thawed and drained

1 small onion, diced

2 garlic cloves, sliced

2 tablespoons butter, melted

1 teaspoon chili powder

½ teaspoon cayenne pepper

½ teaspoon sea salt

⅛ teaspoon freshly ground black pepper

¼ cup heavy (whipping) cream

1 Combine the corn, onion, garlic, butter, chili powder, cayenne pepper, salt, and black pepper in a 6-inch metal bowl that fits into your air fryer basket.

2 Set or preheat the air fryer to 400°F. Place the bowl in the basket and roast for 10 minutes, shaking the basket once during cooking time, until some of the kernels start to turn gold around the edges.

3 Remove the basket and pour the cream over the corn; stir to mix. Return the basket to the air fryer and roast for another 5 minutes or until the cream has thickened slightly. Serve.

SUBSTITUTION TIP: You can omit the cream if you'd like; this corn will still be delicious. If you like things really spicy, add 1 minced chipotle pepper in adobo sauce, and 1 tablespoon adobo sauce to the corn along with the rest of the ingredients.

Cauliflower Quesadillas

FAMILY-FRIENDLY / SERVES 4

PREP TIME:
15 minutes

COOK TIME:
24 minutes

FRY:
375°F

This elegant and delicious recipe starts with cauliflower rice. Buying it fresh or frozen really cuts down on preparation time. The "rice" is cooked until tender in the air fryer, then combined with cheese and spices. Fill tortillas, then air fry until crisp and golden. Serve with a hearty salad for a great meal.

- 1 cup frozen cauliflower rice or fresh riced cauliflower
- 3 tablespoons vegetable broth
- 3 scallions, sliced
- 4 (10-inch) flour tortillas
- 1 cup shredded Havarti cheese
- 1 teaspoon dried oregano
- ½ cup shredded Parmesan cheese
- 1 tablespoon olive oil

PER SERVING:
Calories: 416;
Protein: 18g;
Fat: 21g;
Saturated Fat: 10g;
Carbohydrates: 40g;
Sugar: 3g;
Sodium: 790g;
Fiber: 3g

INGREDIENT TIP: You can make your own cauliflower rice if you'd like. Just rinse a head of cauliflower, break it into florets, and run it through a food processor with the grating blade. You can also grate the cauliflower yourself on a hand grater.

1 Combine the cauliflower rice, vegetable broth, and scallions in a 6-inch metal bowl. Put the bowl in the air fryer basket and the basket in the air fryer.

2 Set or preheat the air fryer to 375°F and cook the cauliflower mixture until tender, 7 to 8 minutes. Drain if necessary.

3 Put the tortillas on the work surface. Put ¼ cup of Havarti cheese on one side of each tortilla, then sprinkle with the oregano. Divide the cauliflower rice mixture over the Havarti and oregano, then sprinkle with the Parmesan cheese. Fold the tortillas in half, enclosing the filling, folding in the edges about 1½ inches.

4 Brush both sides of the tortillas with the olive oil. Place the quesadillas, two at a time, in the air fryer basket. Fry for 6 to 8 minutes, turning the quesadillas over once during cooking time, until crisp, and the cheese is melted.

5 Repeat with remaining quesadillas. Cut each quesadilla into halves to serve.

Sweet Potato Hash Browns

5 INGREDIENTS, GLUTEN-FREE / SERVES 4

PREP TIME:
15 minutes

COOK TIME:
22 minutes

FRY:
400°F

PER SERVING:
Calories: 121;
Protein: 1g;
Fat: 7g;
Saturated Fat: 1g;
Carbohydrates:
14g;
Sugar: 3g;
Sodium: 283g;
Fiber: 2g

Hash browns are a great addition to any meal, but especially breakfast. Sweet potato hash browns are just next level. These tender and crisp hash browns couldn't be simpler. The only real work is shredding the potatoes on a grater. You can flavor these potatoes any way you'd like; this recipe adds chili powder and cumin.

2 medium sweet potatoes, peeled

2 tablespoons olive oil

2 teaspoons chili powder

½ teaspoon ground cumin

½ teaspoon sea salt

⅛ teaspoon cayenne pepper

1 Shred the sweet potatoes on the large side of a grater. Place the shredded potatoes in a bowl of cool water for 10 minutes, then drain well. Pat dry using paper towels.

2 In a large bowl, combine the sweet potatoes, olive oil, chili powder, cumin, salt, and cayenne pepper and toss to coat.

3 Put the seasoned potatoes in the air fryer basket and place the basket in the air fryer.

4 Set or preheat the air fryer to 400°F. Fry for 10 minutes, then remove the basket and shake the potatoes. Return the basket and continue cooking for another 10 to 12 minutes or until the potatoes are crunchy and tender. Serve.

INGREDIENT TIP: You may be able to buy frozen shredded sweet potatoes, or a blend containing sweet potatoes, carrots, and Yukon gold potatoes (Cascadian Farm is one brand), which would work well in this recipe after being thawed and drained. Just make sure you don't buy dried sweet potatoes.

Roasted Five-Spice Broccoli

5 INGREDIENTS, 30 MINUTES, GLUTEN-FREE / SERVES 4

PREP TIME:
10 minutes

COOK TIME:
15 minutes

ROAST:
400°F

PER SERVING:
Calories: 99;
Protein: 3g;
Fat: 7g;
Saturated Fat: 1g;
Carbohydrates: 8g;
Sugar: 2g;
Sodium: 155g;
Fiber: 3g

INGREDIENT TIP:
You can find prepared fresh broccoli florets in the produce aisle of most supermarkets. Use one or two bags in place of the whole bunch of broccoli to save a few minutes prep time.

If you put roasted broccoli in front of people who say they don't like broccoli, you might just convert them. Roasting turns this slightly bitter and sturdy vegetable into a tender and sweet delight, with slightly crisp edges. It's like a completely different veggie. You can roast your broccoli with any spices you'd like; I use Chinese five-spice powder for lots of flavor.

1 bunch fresh broccoli, cut into florets

2 tablespoons olive oil

1 teaspoon five-spice powder

¼ teaspoon onion powder

¼ teaspoon sea salt

⅛ teaspoon freshly ground black pepper

1 Place the broccoli into a large bowl and drizzle with the olive oil. Toss to coat.

2 Sprinkle with the five-spice powder, onion powder, salt, and pepper and toss again.

3 Put the broccoli into the air fryer basket and place the basket in the air fryer.

4 Set or preheat the air fryer to 400°F. Roast the broccoli for 8 minutes. Remove the basket and shake it to redistribute the broccoli. Return the basket and roast for another 5 to 7 minutes until the broccoli is tender with slightly browned edges. Serve immediately.

Mediterranean-Style Veggies

FAMILY-FRIENDLY, GLUTEN-FREE / SERVES 4

PREP TIME:
15 minutes

COOK TIME:
20 minutes

ROAST:
375°F

PER SERVING:
Calories: 142;
Protein: 6g;
Fat: 8g;
Saturated Fat: 1g;
Carbohydrates: 17g;
Sugar: 10g;
Sodium: 255g;
Fiber: 5g

"Mediterranean-style" means that vegetables such as zucchini, mushrooms, and cherry tomatoes are roasted until tender and seasoned with herbs common to the Mediterranean region: basil, thyme, and oregano. This flavorful side dish is simple to make. You can use any of the more tender vegetables such as broccoli, green beans, or leeks with this combination if you'd like.

1½ cups cherry tomatoes

1 yellow bell pepper, sliced

1 small zucchini, sliced

1½ cups button mushrooms, halved lengthwise

2 tablespoons olive oil

1 teaspoon dried basil

½ teaspoon dried oregano

½ teaspoon dried thyme

½ teaspoon garlic powder

½ teaspoon sea salt

⅛ teaspoon freshly ground black pepper

1 Put the tomatoes, bell pepper, zucchini, and mushrooms in the air fryer basket. Drizzle with the olive oil and toss to coat. Then sprinkle with the basil, oregano, thyme, garlic powder, salt, and pepper and toss again. Put the basket in the air fryer.

2 Set or preheat the air fryer to 375°F and roast for 15 to 20 minutes, tossing twice during cooking time, until the vegetables are tender. Serve.

Corn Fritters

FAMILY-FRIENDLY / SERVES 4

PREP TIME:
15 minutes

COOK TIME:
15 minutes
per batch

FRY:
375°F

———————

PER SERVING:
Calories: 122;
Protein: 5g;
Fat: 2g;
Saturated Fat: 1g;
Carbohydrates:
23g;
Sugar: 2g;
Sodium: 266g;
Fiber: 2g

———————

**SUBSTITUTION
TIP:** You can
use just about
any cooked
vegetable to
make fritters
using this
basic recipe.
Try chopped
cooked
well-drained
broccoli,
shredded
drained zuc-
chini, broccoli
slaw, or shred-
ded carrots.

Making corn fritters is one of my favorite ways to serve corn off the cob. These cute little fritters are sweet from the corn and honey, spicy from the chili powder, and crunchy and tender at the same time. I hope your family will love them as much as mine does.

½ cup all-purpose flour

1 teaspoon chili powder

½ teaspoon baking powder

½ teaspoon sea salt

⅛ teaspoon freshly
   ground black pepper

1¼ cups frozen corn kernels,
   thawed and drained

1 large egg, beaten

1 tablespoon honey

1 garlic clove, minced

1 In a medium bowl, combine the flour, chili powder, baking powder, salt, and pepper and mix well.

2 In a small bowl, combine the corn, egg, honey, and garlic and mix well.

3 Add the corn mixture to the flour mixture and stir just until combined. You may need to add more flour to get a thick batter that holds its shape when dropped from a spoon.

4 Line the air fryer basket with parchment paper. Depending on the size of your air fryer, drop two to four ¼-cup measures of the fritter batter onto the paper, 1½ inches apart. Place the basket in the air fryer.

5 Set or preheat the air fryer to 375°F and fry for 10 to 15 minutes, until they are golden brown and hot. Repeat with the remaining batter, if needed. Serve.

Asian-Style Stir-Fry Veggies

30 MINUTES / SERVES 4

PREP TIME:
15 minutes

COOK TIME:
13 minutes

FRY:
400°F

PER SERVING:
Calories: 66;
Protein: 3g;
Fat: 3g;
Saturated Fat: 0g;
Carbohydrates: 9g;
Sugar: 4g;
Sodium: 589g;
Fiber: 1g

INGREDIENT TIP:
If you can't find bok choy, you can substitute Napa cabbage. Shiitakes are the best choice for this recipe, but you can substitute cremini mushrooms if you can't find them.

The Asian-style in this stir-fried recipe comes from the bok choy, shiitake mushrooms, soy sauce, ginger, and hoisin sauce. The glaze combines vegetable broth and cornstarch to add more flavor to the vegetables.

⅓ cup vegetable broth

2 tablespoons low-sodium soy sauce

1 tablespoon hoisin sauce

1 tablespoon cornstarch

1 teaspoon grated fresh ginger

2 teaspoons sesame oil

1 cup broccoli florets

1 cup chopped bok choy (see Tip)

½ cup sliced shiitake mushrooms (see Tip)

1 red bell pepper, sliced

2 garlic cloves, sliced

1 In a small bowl, whisk together the vegetable broth, soy sauce, hoisin sauce, cornstarch, and ginger; set aside.

2 Coat the inside of a 6-inch metal bowl with the sesame oil. Add the broccoli, bok choy, shiitake mushrooms, red bell pepper, and garlic and toss. Put the bowl in the air fryer basket and the basket in the air fryer.

3 Set or preheat the air fryer to 400°F. Fry for 8 to 10 minutes, stirring halfway through cooking time, until the vegetables are crisp-tender.

4 Stir the broth mixture again and add it to the vegetables; stir gently.

5 Continue cooking for another 1 to 3 minutes or until the sauce has thickened. Stir again and serve.

Roasted Italian Bell Peppers

30 MINUTES, FAMILY-FRIENDLY, GLUTEN-FREE / SERVES 4

PREP TIME:
10 minutes

COOK TIME:
11 minutes

ROAST:
350°F

PER SERVING:
Calories: 70;
Protein: 1g;
Fat: 4g;
Saturated Fat: 1g;
Carbohydrates: 9g;
Sugar: 2g;
Sodium: 239g;
Fiber: 1g

When roasted, the flavor and texture of bell peppers changes completely. They become much sweeter and the flesh will develop a velvety texture. Choose a selection of bell pepper colors when you make this recipe for a pretty presentation. These peppers can be used in sandwiches or salads or served as a side dish.

1 red bell pepper, sliced

1 yellow bell pepper, sliced

1 orange bell pepper, sliced

1 tablespoon olive oil

1 teaspoon freshly squeezed lemon juice

1 teaspoon dried Italian seasoning

½ teaspoon sea salt

⅛ teaspoon freshly ground black pepper

¼ cup chopped fresh flat-leaf parsley

1 Combine the bell peppers in the air fryer basket. Drizzle with the olive oil and lemon juice, and sprinkle with the Italian seasoning, salt, and pepper. Toss to coat. Place the basket in the air fryer.

2 Set or preheat the air fryer to 350°F. Roast for 8 to 11 minutes, shaking once during cooking time, until the peppers are tender and starting to brown around the edges. Sprinkle with the parsley and serve.

Tex-Mex Corn and Beans

30 MINUTES, GLUTEN-FREE / SERVES 4

PREP TIME:
10 minutes

COOK TIME:
10 minutes

ROAST:
350°F

PER SERVING:
Calories: 155;
Protein: 7g;
Fat: 4g;
Saturated Fat: 1g;
Carbohydrates:
24g;
Sugar: 3g;
Sodium: 327g;
Fiber: 7g

VARIATION TIP:
To make this
recipe into a
salad, place
the mixture
into a salad
bowl and
add another
tablespoon of
olive oil, ⅓ cup
salsa, and
½ cup grated
queso fresco
or Parmesan
cheese. Toss
and serve with
salad greens.

The combination of corn and beans is a classic in Tex-Mex cooking. This colorful and spicy side dish is perfect when you're serving enchiladas or burritos. In fact, this mixture can be used as a filling for enchiladas by simply adding some cheese and sour cream.

1 (15-ounce) can black beans, drained and rinsed

1 cup frozen corn kernels

1 red bell pepper, seeded and chopped

1 jalapeño pepper, sliced

2 garlic cloves, sliced

1 tablespoon olive oil

1 tablespoon freshly squeezed lime juice

2 teaspoons chili powder

½ teaspoon sea salt

⅛ teaspoon cayenne pepper

1 Combine the black beans, corn, bell pepper, jalapeño pepper, and garlic in the air fryer basket.

2 Drizzle with the olive oil and lime juice and toss to coat. Sprinkle with the chili powder, salt, and cayenne pepper and toss again. Place the basket in the air fryer.

3 Set or preheat the air fryer to 350°F. Roast the vegetables for 10 minutes, shaking the basket halfway through cooking time, until hot and tender. Serve.

Roasted Carrots

5 INGREDIENTS, 30 MINUTES, FAMILY-FRIENDLY, GLUTEN-FREE / SERVES 4

PREP TIME:
5 minutes

COOK TIME:
22 minutes

ROAST:
400°F

PER SERVING:
Calories: 61;
Protein: 1g;
Fat: 3g;
Saturated Fat: 1g;
Carbohydrates: 8g;
Sugar: 4g;
Sodium: 292g;
Fiber: 2g

INGREDIENT TIP:
Did you know that baby carrots are actually large carrots that are bred to be sweeter, then cut down to size? They aren't immature carrots.

Anytime you roast a vegetable, the flavor intensifies, and sweet flavors are brought to the forefront. Because carrots are already sweet, roasting them makes them taste almost like candy. Two types of carrots are roasted in this recipe for visual and textural interest.

2 cups baby carrots

1 large carrot, peeled and sliced ½ inch thick

1 tablespoon freshly squeezed orange juice

2 teaspoons olive oil

1 teaspoon butter, melted

1 teaspoon dried dill weed

½ teaspoon sea salt

⅛ teaspoon freshly ground black pepper

1 Pat the carrots dry with paper towels and place them in the air fryer basket.

2 In a small bowl, combine the orange juice, olive oil, butter, dill weed, salt, and pepper and mix well. Drizzle over the carrots and toss to coat. Place the basket in the air fryer.

3 Set or preheat the air fryer to 400°F. Roast for 10 minutes, then shake the basket and roast for another 8 to 12 minutes or until the carrots are tender and glazed. Serve.

Mushroom Veggie Kabobs

30 MINUTES, FAMILY-FRIENDLY, GLUTEN-FREE / SERVES 4

PREP TIME:
15 minutes

COOK TIME:
11 minutes

ROAST:
400°F

PER SERVING:
Calories: 75;
Protein: 3g;
Fat: 4g;
Saturated Fat: 1g;
Carbohydrates: 9g;
Sugar: 4g;
Sodium: 270g;
Fiber: 2g

Kabobs cook very well in the air fryer, since the appliance mimics the grill. You'll need 6-inch skewers for this recipe; bamboo skewers are easiest to find in this size. Soak them in water for 30 minutes before using them so they won't burn as the veggies cook.

1 (8-ounce) package button mushrooms, rinsed

1 green bell pepper, sliced

1 yellow bell pepper, sliced

1 cup cherry tomatoes

1 tablespoon freshly squeezed lemon juice

1 tablespoon olive oil

2 teaspoons Dijon mustard

½ teaspoon dried marjoram

½ teaspoon sea salt

⅛ teaspoon freshly ground black pepper

1 Build the skewers with the mushrooms, bell peppers, and cherry tomatoes, alternating vegetables for a nice appearance.

2 In a small bowl, whisk together the lemon juice, olive oil, mustard, marjoram, salt, and pepper. Brush this mixture onto the vegetables.

3 Place the skewers in the air fryer basket and put the basket in the air fryer.

4 Set or preheat the air fryer to 400°F. Roast the skewers for 8 to 11 minutes, turning once halfway through cooking time, until the vegetables are tender and starting to brown. Serve.

Roasted Vegetable Salad

30 MINUTES, FAMILY-FRIENDLY, GLUTEN-FREE / SERVES 4

PREP TIME:
15 minutes

COOK TIME:
11 minutes

ROAST:
375°F

PER SERVING:
Calories: 163;
Protein: 3g;
Fat: 14g;
Saturated Fat: 2g;
Carbohydrates: 9g;
Sugar: 5g;
Sodium: 262g;
Fiber: 2g

VARIATION TIP:
Make this salad out of root vegetables instead. Use sliced fennel, baby potatoes, sliced carrots, sliced celeriac, and sliced red onion. The cooking time will increase to 15 to 20 minutes.

A roasted vegetable salad can be served as a side dish or turned into a main dish with the addition of some grilled tofu or cubed cheese. These vegetables are already pretty sweet, but roasting adds tons of flavor and makes the veggies so perfectly tender.

1 yellow summer squash, sliced

1½ cups (2-inch pieces) fresh asparagus

1 orange bell pepper, sliced

1 cup sliced button mushrooms

4 tablespoons olive oil, divided

½ teaspoon sea salt

2 tablespoons freshly squeezed lemon juice

1 tablespoon freshly squeezed orange juice

1 tablespoon honey mustard

1 teaspoon dried thyme

1 Put the squash, asparagus, bell pepper, and mushrooms in the air fryer basket and toss to mix. Drizzle the vegetables with 1 tablespoon of olive oil and sprinkle with the salt. Put the basket in the air fryer.

2 Set or preheat the air fryer to 375°F. Roast for 8 to 11 minutes, tossing halfway through cooking time, until the vegetables are tender.

3 Meanwhile, in a large serving bowl whisk together the remaining 3 tablespoons of olive oil, lemon juice, orange juice, mustard, and thyme.

4 When the vegetables are done, add them to the serving bowl and toss to coat with the dressing. Serve immediately, at room temperature, or chill for a few hours before serving.

Caramelized Sweet Potatoes

5 INGREDIENTS, FAMILY-FRIENDLY, GLUTEN-FREE / SERVES 4

PREP TIME:
15 minutes

COOK TIME:
22 minutes

ROAST:
400°F

PER SERVING:
Calories: 116;
Protein: 1g;
Fat: 3g;
Saturated Fat: 2g;
Carbohydrates:
22g;
Sugar: 11g;
Sodium: 292g;
Fiber: 2g

Everyone is used to having sweet potatoes at Thanksgiving and Christmas, but why not try them other times of the year? This simple and sweet recipe is delicious in spring and summer, too.

2 sweet potatoes

2 tablespoons maple syrup

1 tablespoon butter, melted

1 tablespoon brown sugar

½ teaspoon sea salt

Pinch nutmeg

1 Rinse the sweet potatoes and peel them, then cut into ½-inch cubes. Put the sweet potatoes in the air fryer basket.

2 In a small bowl, combine the maple syrup, butter, brown sugar, salt, and nutmeg and mix well. Drizzle half of this mixture over the sweet potatoes, tossing to coat. Put the basket in the air fryer.

3 Set or preheat the air fryer to 400°F. Roast the potatoes for 10 minutes, then remove the basket from the air fryer, toss the potatoes, and drizzle with the rest of the butter mixture; toss again.

4 Return the basket to the air fryer and continue cooking for another 8 to 12 minutes or until the potatoes are tender and glazed. Serve.

VARIATION TIP: You can make more of the sauce for the potatoes if you'd like. Just double the amount of maple syrup, butter, brown sugar, sea salt, and nutmeg. Use half the mixture to glaze the sweet potatoes as in steps 2 and 3. With the remaining sauce, put a small metal bowl in the air fryer basket and cook for 2 to 3 minutes until bubbly. Put the sweet potatoes in a serving dish and drizzle with the sauce; toss and serve.

Thai-Style Veggie Pizza
PAGE 91

MAINS

Tofu Riblets

PREP TIME:
15 minutes

COOK TIME:
26 minutes

GRILL:
400°F

PER SERVING:
Calories: 209;
Protein: 11g;
Fat: 6g;
Saturated Fat: 0g;
Carbohydrates: 31g;
Sugar: 22g;
Sodium: 808g;
Fiber: 2g

Believe it or not, there's a way to make tofu seem, at least a little bit, like barbecued ribs. The tofu is drained and marinated for a few minutes in a flavorful mixture, then "grilled" in the air fryer until the riblets are crunchy and tender. Serve with some coleslaw and lots of beer or lemonade for a fabulous dinner.

1 (16-ounce) block
  extra-firm tofu
2 tablespoons low-sodium
  soy sauce
1 tablespoon ketchup

1 tablespoon honey
1 cup store-bought
  barbecue
  sauce, divided, plus more
  for serving

1 Drain the tofu, then cut it into 1-by-4-inch slices. Put the slices on layers of paper towel. Put more paper towels on top and press down to remove as much moisture from the tofu as possible. Put the tofu into a glass baking dish.

2 In a small bowl, whisk together the soy sauce, ketchup, and honey. Brush over the tofu on both sides. Set aside for 10 minutes.

3 Put half the tofu slices in the bottom of the air fryer basket. Place a raised rack over the slices and put the remaining tofu slices on it.

4 Set or preheat the air fryer to 400°F. Grill the tofu slices for 10 minutes, turn them over, and grill for another 6 minutes. Remove the tofu from the air fryer.

5 Brush the tofu with ½ cup of the barbecue sauce and put back into the air fryer basket. Grill for 5 minutes. Then turn the tofu, brush with the remaining barbecue sauce, and grill for 4 to 5 minutes or until the tofu is glazed and deep golden brown.

6 Serve the riblets with more barbecue sauce.

Black Bean Burgers

FAMILY-FRIENDLY, GLUTEN-FREE / SERVES 4

PREP TIME:
15 minutes

COOK TIME:
5 minutes, plus another 15 minutes per batch

GRILL:
375°F

———————

PER SERVING:
Calories: 195;
Protein: 9g;
Fat: 9g;
Saturated Fat: 1g;
Carbohydrates: 21g;
Sugar: 2g;
Sodium: 296g;
Fiber: 7g

———————

SUBSTITUTION TIP: If you aren't avoiding gluten, you can use ⅓ cup dried bread crumbs in place of the ground almonds. Or if you can't eat almonds, look for gluten-free bread crumbs at the store.

Black bean burgers are a staple for many vegetarians. But not all black bean burgers are created equal. Some are delicious, others not so much. If you have only purchased commercial black bean burgers and not liked them very much, this recipe just might change your mind. The burgers are crisp on the outside, tender on the inside, and full of flavor.

1 small onion, diced

2 garlic cloves, minced

1 tablespoon olive oil

1 (15-ounce) can black beans, drained and rinsed

⅓ cup ground almonds

1 large egg, beaten

1 tablespoon Worcestershire sauce

1 teaspoon smoked paprika

1 teaspoon ground cumin

½ teaspoon sea salt

⅛ teaspoon freshly ground black pepper

1 Put the onion and garlic in a metal bowl. Drizzle with the olive oil and toss to coat. Place the bowl in the air fryer basket and the basket in the air fryer.

2 Set or preheat the air fryer to 375°F. Grill the vegetables for 3 to 5 minutes or until tender. Remove and put into a large bowl.

3 Add the black beans, ground almonds, egg, Worcestershire sauce, paprika, cumin, salt, and pepper to the bowl and mash using a potato masher until well combined.

4 Form the mixture into four 4-inch patties.

5 Line the air fryer basket with perforated parchment paper. Add the burgers in a single layer, grilling in two batches if needed, and grill for 15 minutes, carefully turning the burgers halfway through cooking time, until they are crisp on the outside.

6 Serve the burgers on sliced buns or sturdy lettuce leaves. Serve with all the usual condiments—mustard, ketchup, pickle relish, cheese, and onions.

Double Mushroom Po' Boy Sandwiches

30 MINUTES, FAMILY-FRIENDLY / SERVES 4

PREP TIME:
15 minutes

COOK TIME:
10 minutes

ROAST:
400°F

───────────────

PER SERVING:
Calories: 302;
Protein: 7g;
Fat: 18g;
Saturated Fat: 3g;
Carbohydrates: 29g;
Sugar: 5g;
Sodium: 712g;
Fiber: 3g

───────────────

INGREDIENT TIP:
Any type of mushroom can be used in this recipe. Try using oyster mushrooms, shiitakes, or just plain old button mushrooms. Any mushroom will have much more flavor if it is well roasted.

When roasted until golden brown, mushrooms take on a very meaty quality. Mushrooms have a flavor called "umami," one of the five tastes your tongue can sense, along with sweet, sour, salty, and bitter. That umami flavor concentrates when the fungi are roasted. Here, the roasted mushrooms are piled onto a toasted bun with salad greens, tomato, and pickles for an outstanding sandwich.

1 tablespoon olive oil

1 tablespoon soy sauce

8 ounces portabella mushrooms, sliced

1 cup sliced cremini mushrooms

½ teaspoon sea salt

4 hoagie rolls, split and toasted

1⅓ cups salad greens

1 large beefsteak tomato, sliced

⅓ cup mayonnaise

¼ cup dill pickle slices

1 In a 6-inch metal bowl, whisk together the olive oil and soy sauce.

2 Add the mushrooms and toss to coat.

3 Set or preheat the air fryer to 400°F. Place the bowl in the air fryer basket. Roast the mushrooms for 10 minutes, stirring the mushrooms with tongs about halfway through cooking time, until they are deep golden brown. Remove the bowl and season the mushrooms with the salt.

4 Make sandwiches by equally splitting the roasted mushrooms among the four rolls and topping them with the salad greens, tomato, mayonnaise, and pickles.

Chickpea Soft Tacos

30 MINUTES, FAMILY-FRIENDLY, GLUTEN-FREE / SERVES 4

PREP TIME:
10 minutes

COOK TIME:
12 minutes

ROAST:
375°F

PER SERVING:
Calories: 316;
Protein: 9g;
Fat: 16g;
Saturated Fat: 3g;
Carbohydrates:
39g;
Sugar: 7g;
Sodium: 482g;
Fiber: 11g

VARIATION TIP:
You can add about ¼ cup of cheese to each of these tacos if you'd like. A good choice is shredded pepper Jack, but you could also use shredded Colby or queso fresco.

Mention vegetarian tacos and some might think they can be boring. Not this recipe! Tender and nutty chickpeas are cooked with onions, red bell pepper, chipotle sauce, lime juice, and spices. Avocados add fabulous texture and flavor and provide a nice temperature contrast with the hot filling.

1 small onion, chopped

1 red bell pepper, sliced

1 tablespoon olive oil

1 (15-ounce) can chickpeas, drained and rinsed

1 chipotle in adobo sauce, minced

1 tablespoon adobo sauce

2 tablespoons freshly squeezed lime juice

1 teaspoon chili powder

½ teaspoon cumin

½ teaspoon sea salt

4 (6-inch) corn tortillas

1 avocado, cubed

1 In a 6-inch metal bowl, combine the onion and bell pepper. Drizzle with the olive oil and toss to coat. Put the bowl in the air fryer basket.

2 Set or preheat the air fryer to 375°F and roast for 2 to 4 minutes or until the vegetables are crisp-tender.

3 Remove the bowl and stir in the chickpeas, chipotle, adobo sauce, lime juice, chili powder, cumin, and salt.

4 Return the bowl to the air fryer and roast for 7 to 8 minutes, stirring once halfway through cooking time, until the ingredients are hot.

5 Fill the tortillas with the chickpea filling and avocado and serve.

Falafel in Pita

SERVES 4

PREP TIME:
15 minutes

COOK TIME:
18 minutes
per batch

FRY:
375°F

PER SERVING:
Calories: 241;
Protein: 12g;
Fat: 11g;
Saturated Fat: 1g;
Carbohydrates:
27g;
Sugar: 7g;
Sodium: 277g;
Fiber: 8g

VARIATION TIP:
You can serve
the little falafel
balls with a
dipping sauce
as an appe-
tizer, too. Try
guacamole
thinned with
a little yogurt
for a fabu-
lous taste
and texture
combination.

A typical falafel is a deep-fried ball made from chickpeas and herbs. Here, I also used ground almonds and then coat the little balls in almond flour to add a nutty flavor. I particularly enjoy these stuffed into pita breads along with fresh veggies and yogurt for a fabulous and healthy sandwich. The peanut butter is added as a substitute for tahini and to add another layer of nutty flavor. To make this gluten-free, skip the pita bread and serve as a salad.

- 1 (15-ounce) can chickpeas, drained and rinsed
- ¼ cup ground almonds
- ¼ cup chopped flat-leaf parsley
- 2 tablespoons chopped fresh cilantro
- 2 tablespoons freshly squeezed lemon juice
- 1 tablespoon peanut butter
- 1 scallion, thinly sliced
- 2 garlic cloves, chopped
- ½ teaspoon sea salt
- ⅛ teaspoon freshly ground black pepper
- ½ cup almond flour
- Cooking oil spray
- 2 pita breads, cut in half and split open
- 1 cup halved cherry tomatoes
- 1 cup sliced seeded cucumber
- ⅓ cup plain Greek yogurt

1. In a blender or food processor, combine the chickpeas, almonds, parsley, cilantro, lemon juice, peanut butter, scallion, garlic, salt, and pepper and blend or pulse until the mixture is ground and combined but is not mushy.

2. Place the almond flour in a shallow bowl.

CONTINUED

3 Using wet hands to prevent sticking, form the chickpea mixture into 2-inch balls. Roll the balls in the almond flour and place in the air fryer basket in a single layer. Spray the tops of the falafel with cooking oil. You may have to cook the falafel in two batches.

4 Set or preheat the air fryer to 375°F. Fry the falafel for 14 to 18 minutes, turning once during cooking time and spraying with more oil, until they are crisp and hot.

5 Make the falafel into sandwiches by placing a few balls each into the pita bread halves with the tomatoes, cucumber, and yogurt. Serve.

Thai-Style Veggie Pizza

FAMILY-FRIENDLY / SERVES 4

PREP TIME:
15 minutes

COOK TIME:
20 minutes

BAKE:
400°F

––––––––––––––––

PER SERVING:
Calories: 402;
Protein: 15g;
Fat: 20g;
Saturated Fat: 4g;
Carbohydrates:
46g;
Sugar: 7g;
Sodium: 616g;
Fiber: 6g

––––––––––––––––

INGREDIENT TIP:
Sometimes
you can find
fresh dough
at the grocery
store, or stop
by a pizza
place and see
if they will sell
you some.

One of the most important ingredients in Thai cooking is peanuts. This interesting pizza starts with a crisp crust, then adds a peanut sauce flavored with sesame oil and lots and lots of veggies. Pizza doesn't have to be made with cheese!

8 ounces frozen pizza dough, thawed, or Pizza Dough (page 126)

⅓ cup peanut butter

3 tablespoons vegetable broth

1 tablespoon soy sauce

1 tablespoon sesame oil

2 teaspoons chili sauce

¼ teaspoon garlic powder

1 cup sliced shiitake mushrooms

⅔ cup shredded carrots

1 yellow bell pepper, thinly sliced

¼ cup chopped salted peanuts

3 scallions, sliced

1 Cut out two rounds of parchment paper that fit into the air fryer basket. Divide the pizza dough in half and roll out each directly onto a round of paper. Place one round in the basket.

2 In a small bowl, whisk together the peanut butter, broth, soy sauce, sesame oil, chili sauce, and garlic powder. Drizzle half this mixture over the dough in the basket.

3 Top the pizza with half of the mushrooms, carrots, bell pepper, peanuts, and scallions. Place the basket in the air fryer.

4 Set or preheat the air fryer to 400°F. Bake for 7 to 10 minutes or until the crust is crisp and the toppings are hot. Remove from the air fryer and place on a wire rack.

5 Repeat with the remaining dough, sauce, and toppings. Cut the pizzas into wedges and serve.

Taco Bowls

30 MINUTES, FAMILY-FRIENDLY, GLUTEN-FREE / SERVES 4

PREP TIME:
15 minutes

COOK TIME:
9 minutes

BAKE:
375°F

———————

PER SERVING:
Calories: 505;
Protein: 20g;
Fat: 21g;
Saturated Fat: 11g;
Carbohydrates:
62g;
Sugar: 4g;
Sodium: 464g;
Fiber: 9g

Bowls are combinations of rice (or other grains) with lots of veggies and a flavorful sauce. This recipe uses Tex-Mex ingredients and flavors to make a slightly spicy taco bowl that is satisfying and delicious.

2 (10-ounce) packages frozen cooked brown rice

1 tablespoon olive oil

1 onion, chopped

3 garlic cloves, minced

1 (15-ounce) can pinto beans, drained and rinsed

1 cup frozen corn kernels

⅔ cup mild salsa, divided

⅓ cup sour cream

2 tablespoons freshly squeezed lime juice

1⅓ cups grated pepper Jack cheese

1 Prepare the rice as directed on the package and set aside.

2 In a 6-inch metal bowl, drizzle the olive oil over the onion and garlic and toss to combine.

3 Set or preheat the air fryer to 375°F. Put the bowl into the air fryer basket. Bake for 3 to 4 minutes or until the vegetables are tender.

4 Remove the basket from the air fryer and add the beans, corn, and ⅓ cup of salsa to the bowl; stir to combine. Return the basket to the air fryer. Bake for another 4 to 5 minutes or until the ingredients are hot.

5 Meanwhile, combine the remaining ⅓ cup of salsa, sour cream, and lime juice in a small bowl until well mixed.

6 Divide the rice equally among four bowls. Divide the bean mixture on top. Drizzle with the sour cream mixture and sprinkle with the cheese. Serve.

Italian Tofu Steaks

5 INGREDIENTS, GLUTEN-FREE / SERVES 4

PREP TIME:
20 minutes

COOK TIME:
20 minutes

BAKE:
375°F

———————

PER SERVING:
Calories: 114;
Protein: 9g;
Fat: 9g;
Saturated Fat: 2g;
Carbohydrates: 2g;
Sugar: 1g;
Sodium: 131g;
Fiber: 1g

Let's face it: Tofu, a mainstay of some vegetarian diets, is pretty bland. But there are things you can do to add flavor to this bean curd, and one of them is to marinate it in a lot of spices just as a meat-eater would marinate a steak. This flavorful marinade adds interest to tofu slices, and the air fryer takes care of the rest by making the tofu crispy and tender.

1 (16-ounce) package firm tofu

1 tablespoon olive oil

1 teaspoon dried Italian seasoning

½ teaspoon smoked paprika

¼ teaspoon garlic powder

¼ teaspoon sea salt

⅛ teaspoon red pepper flakes

1 Drain the liquid from the tofu. Place the tofu on some paper towels. Top with more paper towels and press gently but firmly to remove more liquid. Repeat this step, then cut the tofu into four equal-size slices.

2 In a glass baking dish large enough to hold the tofu slices, whisk together the olive oil, Italian seasoning, paprika, garlic powder, salt, and red pepper flakes. Add the tofu to the dish and turn to coat. Let stand for 10 minutes.

3 Put two of the tofu slices in the air fryer basket. Add a raised rack and put the other two tofu slices on the rack.

4 Set or preheat the air fryer to 375°F. Bake for 15 to 20 minutes or until the tofu is golden brown. Serve.

Mac and Cheese

5 INGREDIENTS, 30 MINUTES, FAMILY-FRIENDLY / SERVES 4

PREP TIME:
5 minutes

COOK TIME:
25 minutes

BAKE:
350°F

———————

PER SERVING:
Calories: 492;
Protein: 26g;
Fat: 29g;
Saturated Fat: 16g;
Carbohydrates:
33g;
Sugar: 8g;
Sodium: 705g;
Fiber: 1g

———————

VARIATION TIP:
Once you
have the basic
recipe down,
change it
to suit your
tastes. Use dif-
ferent cheeses,
such as Colby,
Gruyère,
Muenster,
or Monterey
Jack. Or stir
some cooked
veggies, such
as broccoli
or caramel-
ized onions,
into the mac
and cheese
at the end.

Yes, you can make mac and cheese, including cooking the pasta, in the air fryer. This recipe is simple and fun. Most important, the mac and cheese is delicious. All you need is a 7- or 8-inch round pan that is about 3 inches deep (called a cake barrel or a deep dish). This pan is small enough to fit into the basket, and deep enough to hold the ingredients for this recipe.

1⅔ cups elbow macaroni

2 cups whole milk

2 teaspoons Dijon mustard

1 tablespoon olive oil

1¼ cups shredded Cheddar cheese

1 cup shredded provolone cheese

¼ teaspoon sea salt

⅛ teaspoon freshly ground black pepper

1 Combine the macaroni, milk, mustard, and olive oil in a 7- or 8-inch round pan and stir.

2 Add the Cheddar and provolone cheeses, salt, and pepper and stir again. Put the pan in the air fryer basket.

3 Set or preheat the air fryer to 350°F. Bake for 20 to 25 minutes, stirring twice during cooking time, once at about 7 minutes and again at 13 minutes, until the macaroni is tender.

4 Remove the pan from the air fryer, set on a wire rack, and cover with aluminum foil. Let stand for 5 minutes so the sauce thickens a bit, then stir again and serve.

Mozzarella en Carrozza

30 MINUTES, FAMILY-FRIENDLY / SERVES 4

PREP TIME:
10 minutes

COOK TIME:
18 minutes

BAKE:
400°F

PER SERVING:
Calories: 335;
Protein: 21g;
Fat: 13g;
Saturated Fat: 6g;
Carbohydrates:
34g;
Sugar: 5g;
Sodium: 656g;
Fiber: 5g

Mozzarella en Carrozza translates literally as "mozzarella in a carriage," which means the cheese is enclosed: in bread, in this case. This super simple sandwich is like a grilled cheese, but it's different because the bread is soaked in a custard before being rolled in bread crumbs for a crunchy texture. And it has more added flavor from the sun-dried tomatoes and seasonings.

1⅓ cups shredded mozzarella cheese

¼ cup chopped oil-packed sun-dried tomatoes, drained

8 slices whole-wheat bread

2 large eggs, beaten

⅓ cup whole milk

1 teaspoon dried Italian seasoning

½ cup dried Italian flavored bread crumbs

1 Divide the mozzarella cheese and sun-dried tomatoes among four slices of bread. Top each with a slice of bread. Try to keep the cheese away from the edges of the bread.

2 In a shallow bowl wide enough to hold a sandwich, whisk together the eggs, milk, and Italian seasoning until smooth. Place the bread crumbs in another shallow bowl.

3 Carefully dip the sandwiches into the egg mixture, turning once. Dip each sandwich into the bread crumbs, gently patting the bread crumbs down so they stick to the egg mixture.

4 Set or preheat the air fryer to 400°F. Place two sandwiches in a single layer in the air fryer basket. Bake for 5 minutes, then carefully turn the sandwiches over and bake for another 4 minutes or until the bread is golden and the cheese is melted. Repeat with remaining sandwiches. Cut into halves and serve.

Warm Veggie and Spinach Salad

30 MINUTES, FAMILY-FRIENDLY, GLUTEN-FREE / SERVES 4

PREP TIME:
15 minutes

COOK TIME:
10 minutes

ROAST:
375°F

PER SERVING:
Calories: 247;
Protein: 7g;
Fat: 19g;
Saturated Fat: 4g;
Carbohydrates: 15g;
Sugar: 5g;
Sodium: 266g;
Fiber: 3g

**SUBSTITUTION
TIP:** You can
use any tender
vegetable in
this recipe: Try
zucchini slices,
green beans,
or sliced
mushrooms.
You can also
use another
type of leafy
green, such as
kale, romaine
lettuce, bok
choy, or aru-
gula, in place
of the spinach.

This is a wilted spinach salad, which means that the warm
vegetables and some of the oil the veggies are cooked in are
added to the spinach, which wilts slightly in the heat. That
makes the spinach more tender, and also makes the salad
seem like a complete meal.

⅓ cup mayonnaise

¼ cup buttermilk

1 tablespoon freshly
   squeezed lemon juice

½ teaspoon dried dill

1 red bell pepper, seeded
   and chopped

1 small summer
   squash, sliced

1 cup frozen corn kernels

2 scallions, chopped

2 garlic cloves, sliced

1 tablespoon olive oil

6 cups baby spinach

⅓ cup grated Par-
   mesan cheese

1 In a serving bowl, whisk together the mayonnaise, buttermilk,
lemon juice, and dill. Set aside.

2 Combine the red bell pepper, summer squash, corn, scallions,
and garlic in the air fryer basket. Drizzle with the olive oil and
toss to coat.

3 Set or preheat the air fryer to 375°F. Place the basket in the
air fryer and roast for 10 minutes, shaking the vegetables halfway through cooking time.

4 Put the spinach into the dressing in the serving bowl. Top
with the hot roasted vegetables. Cover the bowl with aluminum foil and let stand for 5 minutes so the spinach wilts.

5 Remove the foil and toss the salad. Top with the Parmesan
cheese and serve.

Rice and Bean–Stuffed Bell Peppers

FAMILY-FRIENDLY, GLUTEN-FREE / SERVES 4

PREP TIME:
20 minutes

COOK TIME:
20 minutes

BAKE:
350°F

PER SERVING:
Calories: 372;
Protein: 19g;
Fat: 12g;
Saturated Fat: 7g;
Carbohydrates:
52g;
Sugar: 9g;
Sodium: 721g;
Fiber: 10g

INGREDIENT TIP:
If you don't want to use frozen precooked rice, you can cook ½ cup of brown rice in 1 cup of water on the stovetop for about 20 to 25 minutes, or until tender. Continue with the recipe.

Stuffed bell peppers is a classic vegetarian main dish. This version is stuffed with rice, black beans, cheese, and veggies to make an easy, comforting, and satisfying meal. Choose bell peppers that will fit snugly into your air fryer basket for this recipe.

- 4 large red bell peppers
- 1 (10-ounce) package frozen cooked brown rice, thawed
- 1 (15-ounce) can black beans, rinsed and drained
- 1 cup frozen corn kernels, thawed
- 1 cup shredded Muenster cheese, divided
- ½ cup salsa
- 3 scallions, chopped
- 2 teaspoons chili powder
- ½ teaspoon ground cumin
- ½ teaspoon sea salt
- ¼ cup grated Parmesan cheese

1. Rinse the peppers and dry them. Cut off the tops and discard them. Remove the membranes and seeds, being careful to not pierce the pepper sides or bottom.

2. In a large bowl, combine the rice, black beans, corn, ½ cup of Muenster cheese, salsa, scallions, chili powder, cumin, and salt and mix well. Stuff the peppers with this mixture, overstuffing them a bit as the filling will shrink as it cooks.

3. Put the peppers in the air fryer basket, nestling them against one another so they stay upright.

4. Set or preheat the air fryer to 350°F. Bake the stuffed peppers for 10 minutes.

5. Top with the remaining ½ cup of Muenster cheese and the Parmesan cheese and continue baking for 5 to 10 minutes or until the peppers are softened, the filling is hot, and the cheese is melted. Serve.

Stuffed Portabella Mushrooms

30 MINUTES, FAMILY-FRIENDLY / SERVES 3

PREP TIME:
15 minutes

COOK TIME:
15 minutes

BAKE:
350°F

PER SERVING:
Calories: 320;
Protein: 19g;
Fat: 22g;
Saturated Fat: 9g;
Carbohydrates: 15g;
Sugar: 4g;
Sodium: 564g;
Fiber: 4g

Portabella mushrooms are quite large, usually 3 to 4 inches round, and perfect for stuffing. The stuffing here is light and flavorful and seasoned with thyme and marjoram. You'll need a raised rack for this recipe to bake six mushrooms at the same time. Two make a light main dish; you can certainly double this recipe if you'd like.

6 (4-inch) portabella mushrooms

2 tablespoons olive oil, divided

1 small onion, chopped

2 garlic cloves, minced

1 cup frozen cut-leaf spinach, thawed and well drained

4 oil-packed sun-dried tomatoes, drained and chopped

½ teaspoon dried thyme

½ teaspoon dried marjoram

¼ teaspoon sea salt

⅛ teaspoon freshly ground black pepper

⅔ cup shredded provolone cheese

⅓ cup ricotta cheese

¼ cup grated Parmesan cheese

1 Rinse the mushrooms briefly under cool running water and pat dry. Carefully pull out the stem from each mushroom and discard.

2 Using a small spoon, gently scrape out the mushroom gills to make more room for the filling. Set aside.

3 In a small saucepan over medium heat, combine 1 tablespoon of the olive oil, the onion, and garlic; cook, stirring often, for about 3 minutes or until crisp-tender.

4 Place the onion and garlic in a medium bowl and add the spinach, tomatoes, thyme, marjoram, salt, and pepper and toss.

5 Stir in the provolone and ricotta cheeses until combined.

6 Fill the mushroom caps with the spinach mixture and sprinkle with the Parmesan cheese.

7 Brush the edges of the mushrooms with the remaining 1 tablespoon of olive oil.

8 Arrange three mushrooms in the air fryer basket. Place the raised rack on top and add the remaining three stuffed mushrooms.

9 Set or preheat the air fryer to 350°F. Bake for 10 to 15 minutes or until the mushrooms are tender and the filling is hot. Serve.

Avocado Veggie Burritos

30 MINUTES, FAMILY-FRIENDLY / SERVES 4

PREP TIME:
15 minutes

COOK TIME:
6 minutes, plus
12 minutes to
heat if desired

ROAST/BAKE:
375°F

PER SERVING:
Calories: 491;
Protein: 18g;
Fat: 28g;
Saturated Fat: 11g;
Carbohydrates:
46g;
Sugar: 9g;
Sodium: 718g;
Fiber: 8g

Burrito, enchilada: What's the difference? Enchiladas are typically baked with a sauce in a casserole, whereas burritos are heated and served without a sauce. That means you can make this recipe ahead of time and refrigerate, and your family can heat them up when they want to eat. The combination of avocados, veggies, and cheese is delicious inside flour tortillas.

1 onion, chopped

1 red bell pepper, chopped

1 tablespoon olive oil

3 plum tomatoes, seeded and chopped

1 cup frozen corn kernels, thawed

2 teaspoons chili powder

½ teaspoon sea salt

⅛ teaspoon freshly ground black pepper

1 avocado, flesh removed

1 tablespoon freshly squeezed lemon juice

4 (8-inch) flour tortillas

1½ cups shredded pepper Jack cheese

1 Combine the onion and red bell pepper in the air fryer basket. Drizzle with the olive oil and toss to coat.

2 Set or preheat the air fryer to 375°F. Roast 4 to 6 minutes, or until the vegetables are tender. Transfer the vegetables to a medium bowl; let the air fryer basket cool for 10 minutes, then rinse out the basket and dry it.

3 Put the tomatoes, corn, chili powder, salt, and pepper in the bowl and mix to combine.

4 In a small bowl, mash the avocado with the lemon juice.

5 Warm the tortillas according to the package directions.

6 Put the tortillas on a work surface. Spread each with the avocado mixture and sprinkle with the cheese. Top with the vegetable mixture.

7 Fold up the bottoms of the tortillas, then fold in the sides and roll up, enclosing the filling.

8 At this point you can serve the burritos as-is or heat them until they are crisp.

9 To heat, set or preheat the air fryer to 375°F. Seal the burritos with a toothpick if necessary. Then place the burritos, seam-side down, in the basket; mist with cooking oil. Bake for 5 minutes, then turn over carefully, mist with oil again, and bake for 4 to 7 minutes more until crisp. Serve.

Roasted Squash Gorgonzola Pizza

5 INGREDIENTS / SERVES 4

PREP TIME:
10 minutes

COOK TIME:
42 minutes

ROAST/BAKE:
400°F

PER SERVING:
Calories: 441;
Protein: 13g;
Fat: 29g;
Saturated Fat: 15g;
Carbohydrates:
32g;
Sugar: 5g;
Sodium: 709g;
Fiber: 3g

Sometimes the simplest pizzas are the best. This flavorful pizza, topped with just roasted squash and Gorgonzola cheese, is incredibly delicious with just five ingredients. This is one of the longer cooking recipes in this book, but the end result is so worth it.

1 (16-ounce) package cubed fresh butternut squash

2 tablespoons olive oil

½ teaspoon sea salt

⅛ teaspoon freshly ground black pepper

1 (8-ounce) package cream cheese, at room temperature

2 tablespoons sour cream

2 (8-inch) round focaccia breads

⅔ cup crumbled gorgonzola cheese

1 Place the squash in the air fryer basket, drizzle with the olive oil, and sprinkle with the salt and pepper. Toss to coat.

2 Set or preheat the air fryer to 400°F. Roast for 15 to 20 minutes, tossing once halfway through cooking time, until the squash is tender and light brown around the edges.

3 Transfer to a bowl. Clean the air fryer basket before you start the pizzas.

4 In a small bowl, combine the cream cheese and sour cream and beat until smooth. Spread this mixture onto the focaccia breads.

5 Divide the roasted squash and the gorgonzola between the two pizzas. Working in batches, place one pizza in the air fryer basket.

6 Set or preheat the air fryer to 400°F. Bake for 7 to 11 minutes or until the crust is crisp and the pizza is hot. Repeat with remaining pizza. Serve hot.

INGREDIENT TIP: Boboli is a brand of focaccia that comes in an 8-inch round and can be used as a pizza base. Your local grocery store or bakery may sell flatbread in this size, too.

Apple Berry
Crumble
PAGE 107

CHAPTER SIX

DESSERTS & STAPLES

Peanut Butter Brownies

30 MINUTES, FAMILY-FRIENDLY / SERVES 8

PREP TIME:
10 minutes

COOK TIME:
16 minutes

BAKE:
325°F

PER SERVING:
Calories: 169;
Protein: 4g;
Fat: 11g;
Saturated Fat: 4g;
Carbohydrates: 15g;
Sugar: 10g;
Sodium: 112g;
Fiber: 1g

VARIATION TIP:
Frost these brownies by melting ¾ cup of semisweet chocolate chips with 3 tablespoons peanut butter in a small saucepan. Pour over the brownies while they are still warm and spread to cover. Let cool before cutting and serving.

All brownies are delicious, of course, but using peanut butter really makes these brownies chewy and moist. Brownies bake beautifully in the air fryer. You can use chunky or smooth peanut butter to make these treats.

½ cup brown sugar

¼ cup peanut butter

3 tablespoons butter, melted

1 large egg

1 teaspoon vanilla

⅓ cup all-purpose flour

⅛ teaspoon baking powder

Pinch sea salt

Nonstick baking spray containing flour

3 tablespoons chopped salted peanuts

1 In a medium bowl, combine the brown sugar, peanut butter, and butter and mix well. Add the egg and vanilla and beat to combine.

2 Stir in the flour, baking powder, and salt just until combined.

3 Spray a 6-inch round pan with the baking spray. Spread the batter into the pan. Sprinkle with the peanuts.

4 Set or preheat the air fryer to 325°F. Place the pan in the air fryer basket and bake for 13 to 16 minutes or until the brownies look set and a toothpick inserted near the center comes out with only a few moist crumbs.

5 Place the pan on a wire rack to cool. Cut the brownies into wedges to serve.

Apple Berry Crumble

FAMILY-FRIENDLY / SERVES 4

PREP TIME:
15 minutes

COOK TIME:
20 minutes

BAKE:
325°F

PER SERVING:
Calories: 278;
Protein: 3g;
Fat: 13g;
Saturated Fat: 7g;
Carbohydrates:
41g;
Sugar: 25g;
Sodium: 146g;
Fiber: 4g

**SUBSTITUTION
TIP:** You
can make
this recipe
gluten-free by
omitting the
all-purpose
flour in the
topping
and using a
gluten-free
flour blend
or ground
almonds.
Make sure the
rolled oats
are gluten-
free, too.

Crisps, crumbles, grunts, and cobblers: All of these desserts use fruit with some type of topping. Crisps and crumbles are similar, with a streusel topping, although a crumble topping doesn't have nuts. Grunts and cobblers are made with batter poured over the fruit. Serve this crumble warm from the air fryer with some vanilla ice cream on the side.

1 large Granny Smith apple, peeled and chopped

½ cup chopped strawberries

⅓ cup raspberries

1 tablespoon freshly squeezed lemon juice

2 tablespoons granulated sugar

½ cup rolled oats

⅓ cup brown sugar

¼ cup butter, at room temperature

¼ cup all-purpose flour

½ teaspoon cinnamon

Pinch sea salt

1 In a 7-inch round pan, combine the apple, strawberries, and raspberries. Drizzle with the lemon juice, then sprinkle with the sugar and toss to mix.

2 In a medium bowl, combine the oats, brown sugar, butter, flour, cinnamon, and salt and mix until crumbly, like coarse sand.

3 Sprinkle the oat mixture over the fruit in the pan.

4 Set or preheat the air fryer to 325°F. Put the pan in the air fryer basket. Bake for 15 to 20 minutes, checking after 15 minutes, until the fruit is bubbling and the topping is golden brown. Let cool for 20 minutes, then serve.

Jumbo Candy Bar Cookie

FAMILY-FRIENDLY / SERVES 4

PREP TIME:
15 minutes

COOK TIME:
18 minutes

BAKE:
350°F

PER SERVING:
Calories: 132;
Protein: 2g;
Fat: 7g;
Saturated Fat: 4g;
Carbohydrates:
16g;
Sugar: 8g;
Sodium: 87g;
Fiber: 1g

There's something so fun about serving one big cookie that everybody gets to eat. This tender and chewy peanut butter cookie is filled with sliced candy bars that melt as the cookie bakes. The only trick to this recipe is to make sure all the candy is covered with dough, so it stays inside the cookie!

½ cup brown sugar

⅓ cup butter, at room temperature

1 large egg

1 teaspoon vanilla

1 cup all-purpose flour

½ teaspoon baking powder

¼ teaspoon sea salt

Nonstick baking spray containing flour

5 fun size chocolate, nut, and caramel candy bars

1 In a medium bowl, combine the brown sugar, butter, egg, and vanilla and mix well.

2 Add the flour, baking powder, and salt and mix just until a dough forms.

3 Spray a 7-inch round pan with the baking spray, line with parchment paper on the bottom, and spray the paper.

4 Divide the dough in half. Put half of the dough into the pan and spread out to the edges, patting gently.

5 Slice the candy bars into ½-inch pieces and put them on the dough in the pan, keeping them away from the edges.

6 Top the candy bar slices with the remaining dough and smooth out, being sure to cover all of the candy. Press down on the edges lightly to make sure the dough is sealed.

7 Set or preheat the air fryer to 350°F. Put the pan in the air fryer basket. Bake for 13 to 18 minutes, checking after 13 minutes, until the cookie is golden brown and set.

8 Take the basket out of the air fryer, then carefully remove the pan and cool on a wire rack for 10 to 15 minutes before you attempt to remove the cookie. Serve whole. Let people break off pieces to eat.

Pear Pecan Crostata

5 INGREDIENTS, FAMILY-FRIENDLY / SERVES 4

PREP TIME:
15 minutes

COOK TIME:
24 minutes

BAKE:
350°F

———————

PER SERVING:
Calories: 418;
Protein: 4g;
Fat: 27g;
Saturated Fat: 3g;
Carbohydrates:
45g;
Sugar: 18g;
Sodium: 247g;
Fiber: 6g

A crostata is a freeform pie that's perfect for people who are new to making or using pie crusts. You can use a purchased pie crust or make your own (see page 128). The crust is fitted into a springform pan and topped with the filling, then the edges of the crust are folded over the filling, leaving the filling exposed in the center. Bosc or Anjou pears work nicely here. This simple recipe is really delicious and easy.

2 ripe pears, peeled, cored, and chopped

⅔ cup coarsely chopped pecans

2 tablespoons granulated sugar

1 tablespoon all-purpose flour

1 (11-inch) round pie crust

1 In a medium bowl, combine the pears and pecans. Sprinkle with the sugar and flour and toss gently to coat.

2 Ease the pie crust into a 7-inch springform pan. Press the crust down onto the bottom of the pan and up the sides.

3 Spoon the pear filling into the crust, spreading it evenly.

4 Gently pull the sides of the crust down over the filling, pleating the crust as you work, leaving the center of the filling uncovered.

5 Set or preheat the air fryer to 350°F. Using a foil sling, lower the springform pan into the basket in the air fryer. Bake for 18 to 24 minutes or until the pears are tender and bubbling slightly, and the crust is light golden brown.

6 Using the foil sling, remove the pan from the basket and let cool on a wire rack for about 20 minutes. Remove the sides of the pan and slice the crostata into wedges to serve.

SUBSTITUTION TIP: You can make this recipe with just about any fruit and nut combination. Use apricots and pistachios, or apples and walnuts, or even try peaches with chopped macadamia nuts.

Gingerbread Meringue-Crusted Nuts

30 MINUTES, FAMILY-FRIENDLY, GLUTEN-FREE / SERVES 8 TO 10

PREP TIME:
15 minutes

COOK TIME:
15 minutes

BAKE:
300°F

PER SERVING:
Calories: 319;
Protein: 4g;
Fat: 27g;
Saturated Fat: 4g;
Carbohydrates:
19g;
Sugar: 15g;
Sodium: 58g;
Fiber: 4g

**SUBSTITUTION
TIP:** You can
use other
nuts in this
recipe or try a
combination.
Good choices
include whole
cashews,
walnuts, or
macada-
mia nuts.

These nuts, which are coated with a gingerbread-flavored meringue, are the perfect dessert after a big meal. They will satisfy any sweet craving. This type of recipe takes an hour to bake in the oven. The air fryer makes it in a fraction of the time! The meringue browns and becomes crisp and the nuts toast. Just be sure to stir every 5 minutes while the nuts are cooking for a delicious and easy treat.

1 large egg white

Pinch sea salt

⅓ cup granulated sugar

⅓ cup brown sugar

½ teaspoon cinnamon

½ teaspoon ground ginger

⅛ teaspoon nutmeg

2½ cups small whole pecans

2 tablespoons
  butter, melted

1 In a medium bowl, use a hand mixer to beat the egg white and salt until foamy.

2 Gradually beat in the granulated and brown sugars until the mixture starts to stiffen. Beat in the cinnamon, ginger, and nutmeg.

3 Fold the pecans into the meringue.

4 Line the air fryer basket with parchment paper.

5 Spread one-third of the nuts in an even layer in the basket and drizzle some butter on top. Repeat twice, making three layers of nuts and three layers of butter.

6 Set or preheat the air fryer to 300°F. Bake for 5 minutes, then remove basket and stir the nuts. Bake for 5 minutes longer, then stir again. Finally, bake for another 5 minutes or until the nuts are toasted and light brown.

7 Spread the nuts on a sheet of parchment paper and let stand for 1 hour. The nuts will be crisp. Store in an airtight container at room temperature for up to 3 days.

AIR FRYER TIP: Be sure to immediately soak the air fryer basket in warm water once the nuts are removed to make cleanup easier. Some of the meringue may stick to the basket, but soaking it in water for an hour or two will loosen the meringue, making it much easier to clean.

White Chocolate Blondies

FAMILY-FRIENDLY / SERVES 6

PREP TIME:
15 minutes

COOK TIME:
20 minutes

BAKE:
325°F

PER SERVING:
Calories: 430;
Protein: 5g;
Fat: 22g;
Saturated Fat: 13g;
Carbohydrates:
56g;
Sugar: 38g; Sodium: 110g; Fiber: 1g

INGREDIENT TIP:
You can save the extra egg white from this recipe to make the Sweet Potato Tots (page 57) or Gingerbread Meringue–Crusted Nuts (page 112). Egg whites freeze very well, too. To thaw, just let them sit in the refrigerator overnight.

White chocolate is used to make these wonderful blondies instead of regular chocolate, and semisweet chocolate is drizzled on top for contrast.

⅔ cup white chocolate chips

⅓ cup butter

½ cup brown sugar

¼ cup granulated sugar

1 large egg

1 large egg yolk

1 teaspoon vanilla

1 cup all-purpose flour

⅛ teaspoon sea salt

Unsalted butter, at room temperature

⅓ cup semisweet chocolate chips

1 In a small saucepan over low heat, melt the white chocolate chips and butter together, stirring frequently until melted and combined, 4 to 5 minutes.

2 Transfer the mixture to a medium bowl. Add the brown and granulated sugars and beat well. Then add the egg, egg yolk, and vanilla and beat until smooth.

3 Stir in the flour and salt until just combined.

4 Grease a 7-inch springform pan with the unsalted butter. Cut out a piece of parchment paper to fit inside the pan and grease the paper, too.

5 Pour the batter into the pan and smooth the top.

6 Set or preheat the air fryer to 325°F. Place the pan in the air fryer basket. Bake for 15 to 20 minutes, or until a toothpick inserted near the center of the brownies comes out with only a few moist crumbs.

7 Remove the pan and let cool completely on a wire rack.

8 Melt the dark chocolate chips as directed on the package and drizzle on top.

Pistachio Baked Pears

5 INGREDIENTS, 30 MINUTES, FAMILY-FRIENDLY, GLUTEN-FREE / SERVES 4

PREP TIME:
10 minutes

COOK TIME:
14 minutes

BAKE:
350°F

PER SERVING:
Calories: 180;
Protein: 2g;
Fat: 9g;
Saturated Fat: 4g;
Carbohydrates:
25g;
Sugar: 17 g;
Sodium: 103g;
Fiber: 4g

**SUBSTITUTION
TIP:** You can
bake apples
using this
method, too.
Because pears
are softer,
the apples
will bake
5 to 10 minutes
longer,
until they
are tender.

Baked fruit is a really wonderful and simple dessert. Baking caramelizes the sugars in the fruit, especially near the surface, which creates delicious and complex compounds that only appear when the fruit is hot. Serve with some vanilla or caramel ice cream for a perfect end to a meal.

2 large ripe pears
(Bosc or Anjou)

2 tablespoons
butter, melted

3 tablespoons brown sugar

⅛ teaspoon cinnamon

½ cup whole unsalted
shelled pistachios

Pinch sea salt

1 Cut the pears in half lengthwise, leaving the stems on one half of each pear. Carefully remove the seeds using a melon baller or spoon.

2 Put the pears into the air fryer basket, cut-side up. Brush the pears with the melted butter, then sprinkle with the brown sugar and cinnamon.

3 Set or preheat the air fryer to 350°F. Bake for 8 minutes, then remove the basket from the air fryer.

4 Sprinkle the pears with the pistachios, concentrating them in the hollow where the seeds were. Sprinkle with the salt.

5 Return the basket to the air fryer. Bake for another 3 to 6 minutes or until the pears are tender and glazed. Serve.

Bread Pudding with Dried Fruits

FAMILY-FRIENDLY / SERVES 4

PREP TIME:
20 minutes

COOK TIME:
35 minutes

BAKE:
350°F

PER SERVING:
Calories: 481;
Protein: 8g;
Fat: 30g;
Saturated Fat: 17g;
Carbohydrates:
48g;
Sugar: 31g;
Sodium: 323g;
Fiber: 3g

Bread pudding is the ultimate comfort food. Bread cubes are soaked in an egg custard, absorbing the mixture, then baked until the top is crisp and brown and the inside is still soft and custardy. This recipe is made with dried fruits for color and delicious flavor. Serve with some soft vanilla ice cream or caramel sauce.

¾ **cup heavy (whipping) cream**

½ **cup whole milk**

¼ **cup brown sugar**

2 **large egg yolks**

3 **tablespoons butter, melted**

2 **tablespoons honey**

1 **teaspoon vanilla**

Pinch sea salt

4 **cups bread cubes**

¼ **cup dried cranberries**

¼ **cup golden raisins**

Unsalted butter, at room temperature

1 In a large bowl, combine the cream, milk, brown sugar, egg yolks, butter, honey, vanilla, and salt and mix well.

2 Stir in the bread cubes. Stir in the cranberries and raisins. Let stand for 15 minutes.

3 Grease the bottom and sides of a 7-inch springform pan with the unsalted butter. Add the bread mixture.

4 Set or preheat the air fryer to 350°F. Put the pan in the air fryer basket. Bake for 30 to 35 minutes or until the bread pudding is set and golden brown on top.

5 Remove from the air fryer and cool for 20 minutes, then serve.

Raspberry Chocolate Lava Cake

30 MINUTES, FAMILY-FRIENDLY / SERVES 4

PREP TIME:
15 minutes

COOK TIME:
12 minutes per batch

BAKE:
375°F

PER SERVING:
Calories: 452;
Protein: 6g;
Fat: 25g;
Saturated Fat: 15g;
Carbohydrates: 55g;
Sugar: 41g;
Sodium: 189g;
Fiber: 4g

Lava cakes, also called molten chocolate cakes, have a soft filling. They are made with more chocolate and egg than an average cake, so the center never bakes completely. The result is a wonderful gooey filling. These cakes are perfect for a special occasion.

⅓ cup semisweet chocolate chips

¼ cup milk chocolate chips

¼ cup butter

2 large eggs

1 large egg yolk

¼ cup granulated sugar

3 tablespoons powdered sugar

1 teaspoon vanilla

4 tablespoons all-purpose flour

¼ teaspoon baking powder

Pinch sea salt

Unsalted butter, at room temperature

2 teaspoons cocoa powder

4 teaspoons raspberry jam

1 cup fresh raspberries

1 tablespoon freshly squeezed lemon juice

1 In a small microwave-safe bowl, melt the semisweet chocolate chips, milk chocolate chips, and butter in the microwave on medium power, 2 to 3 minutes. Remove and stir until combined and smooth, then set aside.

2 In a medium bowl, beat together the eggs and egg yolk. Gradually add the granulated and powdered sugars, beating until the mixture is fluffy and lighter yellow in color. Beat in the vanilla.

3 Add the flour, baking powder, and salt and mix until combined. Then fold in the chocolate and butter mixture.

4 Grease four 4-ounce glass heatproof ramekins with the unsalted butter. Sprinkle ½ teaspoon cocoa power in each ramekin and shake to coat. Shake out the excess cocoa powder.

5 Fill the ramekins half full with the batter. Top each with a teaspoon of the raspberry jam. Cover the jam with the rest of the batter.

6 Place the ramekins in the air fryer basket. You may be able to bake all four at one time, or just two at a time, depending on the size of your machine.

7 Set or preheat the air fryer to 375°F. Put the basket in the air fryer. Bake for 9 to 12 minutes or until the edges of the cake are set; the center will still be jiggly.

8 While the cakes are baking, place the raspberries and lemon juice in a small saucepan. Bring to a simmer over medium-low heat. Simmer for 2 to 4 minutes or until a sauce forms. Remove from heat and set aside.

9 Remove the basket from the air fryer and let the ramekins cool on a wire rack for 5 minutes. Run a knife around the edge of each ramekin and invert each cake onto a serving plate. Top with the sauce and serve.

Berry Pavlova

FAMILY-FRIENDLY, GLUTEN-FREE / SERVES 4

PREP TIME:
10 minutes

COOK TIME:
45 minutes

BAKE:
300°F

PER SERVING:
Calories: 280;
Protein: 4g;
Fat: 11g;
Saturated Fat: 7g;
Carbohydrates:
44g;
Sugar: 41g;
Sodium: 95g;
Fiber: 1g

INGREDIENT TIP:
Egg whites will
not beat to
peaks if there
is even the
tiniest bit of oil
or egg yolk in
them. Be very
careful when
you separate
the whites
from the yolks.
And use a very
clean bowl to
get the best
volume from
the egg whites.

A pavlova is a large meringue that is crisp on the outside and soft like a marshmallow on the inside. It is named after Anna Pavlova, a Russian ballerina, to mimic her white fluffy tutu. This pavlova is covered with whipped cream and fruit and makes a lovely dessert.

3 large egg whites
Pinch sea salt
⅔ cup granulated sugar
1 teaspoon cornstarch
1 teaspoon apple cider vinegar
½ cup heavy (whipping) cream

2 tablespoons powdered sugar
⅓ cup blueberries
⅓ cup raspberries
⅓ cup chopped strawberries
1 teaspoon honey

1 In a very clean mixing bowl, use a hand mixer to beat the egg whites and salt.

2 When soft peaks start to form, beat in the granulated sugar, one tablespoon at a time. Keep beating until the meringue is glossy and forms stiff peaks when the beater is lifted.

3 Fold in the cornstarch and vinegar.

4 Cut a piece of parchment paper the same size as the bottom of a 7-inch round pan. Put a dot of the meringue mixture on the bottom of the pan and add the parchment paper; this helps the paper stay in place.

5 Put the meringue mixture on the parchment paper, forming it into a disc and flattening the top and sides with a spatula.

6 Set or preheat the air fryer to 300°F. Place the pan in the air fryer basket and the basket in the air fryer and bake for 40 to 45 minutes or until the meringue is dry to the touch. Turn off the air fryer, pull the basket out about an inch, and let the meringue cool for 1 hour.

7 Remove the meringue from the air fryer and cool completely on a wire rack.

8 In a small bowl, beat the cream with the powdered sugar until soft peaks form.

9 Turn the meringue over so the bottom is on top. Spread the cream over the meringue, then top with the blueberries, raspberries, and strawberries and drizzle with the honey. You can serve this immediately or cover and refrigerate for up to 1 day.

Gingerbread

FAMILY-FRIENDLY / SERVES 6

PREP TIME:
15 minutes

COOK TIME:
27 minutes

BAKE:
325°F

PER SERVING:
Calories: 181;
Protein: 3g;
Fat: 1g;
Saturated Fat: 1g;
Carbohydrates:
41g;
Sugar: 24g;
Sodium: 193g;
Fiber: 1g

Gingerbread is such an old-fashioned treat that people don't seem to make much of it anymore. I'm not sure why because it's delicious and comforting and fills your home with wonderful aromas. This recipe uses honey instead of molasses for a milder taste that kids will like. Serve it warm with caramel sauce on a cold winter day.

1 cup all-purpose flour

1 teaspoon ground ginger

½ teaspoon cinnamon

½ teaspoon baking soda

¼ teaspoon sea salt

⅛ teaspoon nutmeg

⅛ teaspoon ground cardamom

⅓ cup brown sugar

⅓ cup honey

⅓ cup milk

1 large egg yolk

Unsalted butter, at room temperature

1 In a medium bowl, combine the flour, ginger, cinnamon, baking soda, salt, nutmeg, and cardamom and mix well.

2 In another medium bowl, combine the brown sugar, honey, milk, and egg yolk and beat until combined.

3 Stir the honey mixture into the flour mixture just until combined.

4 Grease a 7-by-3-inch round pan with the unsalted butter. Cut a piece of parchment paper to fit the bottom of the pan, and grease that. Pour in the batter. Cover the pan tightly with aluminum foil and poke a few holes in the foil with the tip of a knife.

5 Set or preheat the air fryer to 325°F. Put the pan in the air fryer basket. Bake for 22 to 27 minutes or until a toothpick inserted near the center of the gingerbread comes out with only a few moist crumbs.

6 Remove from the air fryer and cool on a wire rack for 20 minutes, then cut into wedges to serve.

Fruit-Filled Cream Puffs

FAMILY-FRIENDLY / SERVES 6

PREP TIME:
15 minutes

COOK TIME:
24 minutes
per batch

BAKE:
400°F

_____

PER SERVING:
Calories: 151;
Protein: 4g;
Fat: 10g;
Saturated Fat: 5g;
Carbohydrates:
14g;
Sugar: 4g;
Sodium: 118g;
Fiber: 1g

_____

SUBSTITUTION TIP: You can fill these cream puffs with ice cream, flavored whipped cream, or even pudding if you'd like. Or offer your guests a choice; put out several fillings and let them create their own dessert.

Cream puffs are very easy to make in the air fryer. The eggs are thoroughly beaten into a thick batter to add air and protein, so these little treats rise and puff very quickly in the air fryer's swirling heat. Then they are filled with fresh fruit.

½ **cup raspberries**

¼ **cup chopped strawberries**

¼ **cup blueberries**

1 **tablespoon honey**

6 **tablespoons water**

¼ **cup butter**

½ **cup all-purpose flour**

Pinch sea salt

2 **large eggs**

1 Combine the raspberries, strawberries, and blueberries with the honey in a small bowl and mix gently; set aside.

2 Combine the water and butter in a medium saucepan over high heat and bring to a rolling boil. Reduce the heat to medium and add the flour and salt. Beat well until the dough forms a ball and pulls away from the sides of the pan.

3 Remove the pan from the heat. Using an electric hand mixer, beat in the eggs, one at a time, until the dough is smooth and shiny.

4 Line a 7-inch round cookie sheet with parchment paper. Working in batches, spoon three rounded tablespoons of the dough onto the cookie sheet (half the dough), 1 inch apart.

5 Set or preheat the air fryer to 400°F. Put the cookie sheet in the air fryer basket. Bake for 18 to 24 minutes or until the cream puffs are puffed and golden brown. Remove the cream puffs and let cool on a wire rack. Repeat with remaining dough.

6 Slice the cream puffs in half crosswise. Remove any loose strands of dough, and fill with the fruit.

Peppermint Bonbon Baked Alaska

FAMILY-FRIENDLY / SERVE 4

PREP TIME:
25 minutes, plus 6 hours to freeze

COOK TIME:
20 minutes

BAKE:
325°F, then 400°F

_____

PER SERVING:
Calories: 403;
Protein: 7g;
Fat: 17g;
Saturated Fat: 10g;
Carbohydrates: 58g;
Sugar: 42g;
Sodium: 202g;
Fiber: 3g

This recipe is a showstopper! It's made in three parts. First, you make the brownie bottom. Then, you add the ice cream dome, which is frozen until firm. Finally, you make meringue, "frost" the brownie and ice cream, and bake again for just a few minutes until the meringue is golden brown.

¼ cup plus ⅓ cup granulated sugar, divided

¼ cup butter, melted

¼ cup brown sugar

2 large eggs, yolks and whites separated

1 teaspoon vanilla

½ cup all-purpose flour

¼ cup cocoa powder

Pinch sea salt

Unsalted butter, at room temperature

2 cups mint ice cream with chocolate chips

1 In a medium bowl, combine ¼ cup of granulated sugar, the butter, and brown sugar and mix well. Beat in the egg yolks and vanilla.

2 Add the flour, cocoa powder, and salt and mix just until combined. Cover and refrigerate the egg whites.

3 Grease a 6-by-2-inch round pan with the unsalted butter. Cut a piece of parchment paper to fit the bottom of the pan and grease it. Pour the brownie batter into the pan. Cover the pan with aluminum foil, crimping the edges to secure. Poke a few holes in the foil with the tip of a knife.

4 Set or preheat the air fryer to 325°F. Put the pan in the air fryer basket. Bake for 12 to 17 minutes or until a toothpick inserted near the center comes out with only a few moist crumbs.

5 Remove the pan from the air fryer and cool for 20 minutes on a wire rack, then run a knife around the edges of the pan and invert the brownie onto the rack. Cool completely.

6   Line a 5-inch bowl with plastic wrap. Add the ice cream, pressing to fit the bowl. Smooth the flat surface of the ice cream.

7   Put the brownie on a 7-inch round cookie sheet, or in a 7-inch springform pan.

8   Invert the bowl onto the center of the brownie, pressing down gently so the ice cream adheres to the brownie. Leave the plastic wrap around the ice cream. Cover the ice cream and brownie and freeze for at least 3 hours.

9   While the ice cream and brownie freeze, make the meringue. In a very clean medium bowl, beat the cold egg whites until frothy. Gradually add the remaining ⅓ cup of sugar, beating until stiff peaks form.

10   Remove the brownie and ice cream from the freezer. Remove the plastic. Carefully "frost" the whole thing with the meringue, just barely covering the brownie part, but frosting the ice cream thickly. Make swirls with your knife.

11   Freeze again, uncovered, for at least 3 hours. When it's frozen solid, you can carefully cover it with plastic wrap. Remove the plastic before baking.

12   When you're ready to eat, set or preheat the air fryer to 400°F. Lower the cookie sheet or pan into the air fryer basket using a foil sling or plate gripper. Bake for 2 to 3 minutes or until the meringue is golden brown in spots. Carefully lift the dessert out of the air fryer using tongs to grip the foil sling or using the plate gripper. Cut into fourths and serve immediately.

COOKING TIP: This recipe may seem complicated, but each step is simple. Keep this dessert in the freezer for up to 3 months and take it out when you really want to impress guests.

INGREDIENT TIP: Mint ice cream with chocolate chips is called "Peppermint Bonbon Ice Cream" in the upper Midwest.

Bread Rolls or Pizza Dough

FAMILY-FRIENDLY / MAKES 21 ROLLS OR DOUGH FOR 2 PIZZAS

PREP TIME:
1 hour 45 minutes

COOK TIME:
16 minutes

BAKE:
325°F

PER SERVING:
Calories: 372;
Protein: 11g;
Fat: 10g;
Saturated Fat: 5g;
Carbohydrates: 59g;
Sugar: 4g;
Sodium: 215g;
Fiber: 2g

Having bread dough (that you can use for pizza) in your freezer is a real time-saver. You do, of course, have to plan ahead of time and move it from the freezer to the refrigerator the night before, but that's a simple step. This dough can be used to make Thai-Style Veggie Pizza (page 91) or any pizza you'd like, as well as dinner rolls or bread. Half of this recipe is one pound of bread dough.

3 cups all-purpose flour, plus additional for dusting

1 cup bread flour

3 teaspoons instant dry yeast

1 tablespoon granulated sugar

½ teaspoon sea salt

1 cup whole milk

¼ cup butter

2 large eggs

Vegetable oil

1 In a large bowl, combine the all-purpose and bread flours. Stir in the yeast, sugar, and salt.

2 In a medium saucepan over low heat, combine the milk and butter. Heat until the butter melts, 4 to 6 minutes. Stir.

3 Combine the milk mixture with the flour mixture. Add the eggs and beat well. Keep stirring until a dough forms.

4 Lightly dust a work surface with all-purpose flour. Turn the dough onto the work surface and knead with your hands (fold the dough over and push it back and forth to help develop the gluten) until it is smooth, about 5 minutes.

5 Coat a large mixing bowl with the oil. Put the dough into the bowl. Turn the dough in the oil to coat it. Cover with a kitchen towel and let rise for 1 hour 30 minutes. It should double in volume.

6 Punch down the dough, then divide into three parts if making rolls, or two parts if making pizza. Put each part into its own freezer bag labeled with the date and name. Freeze for up to 2 months.

7 To use, thaw the dough in the refrigerator overnight and proceed with the recipe.

8 **To make rolls:** Divide a one-third portion of dough into 7 balls. Line the air fryer basket with parchment paper and add the dough balls in a single layer. Cover the basket with a kitchen towel and let rise for 45 minutes.

9 Set or preheat the air fryer to 325°F. Bake for 12 to 16 minutes or until the rolls are light golden brown. Let cool on wire racks. Repeat with other portions of dough as desired.

10 **To make pizza:** Cut out a round of parchment paper that fits into the air fryer basket. Roll out one half of the dough directly onto the round of paper. Place round in the basket. Top pizza dough as desired.

11 Set or preheat the air fryer to 400°F. Bake for 7 to 10 minutes or until the crust is crisp and the toppings are hot. Remove from the air fryer and place on a wire rack. Repeat with second half of dough.

INGREDIENT TIP: Bread flour is made from higher protein wheat, so it has more gluten. Adding bread flour to doughs makes the dough lighter with a more developed crumb (interior). The bread rises higher and has better texture, too. One package of dry yeast contains 2½ teaspoons, so you'll need more than one package for this recipe; this is necessary to make sure the dough has enough yeast to rise after it's frozen. Leftover yeast can be frozen, too.

Pie Crust

PREP TIME:
**20 minutes,
plus 20 min-
utes to freeze**

COOK TIME:
10 minutes

BAKE:
350°F

———————

**PER SERVING
(1/4 CRUST):**
Calories: 317;
Protein: 4g;
Fat: 23g;
Saturated Fat: 8g;
Carbohydrates:
24g;
Sugar: 0g;
Sodium: 118g;
Fiber: 1g

Homemade pie crust is simple once you know a few tricks. Master this recipe and you won't ever have to buy premade pie crust again, which doesn't taste as good anyway! The tricks are to handle the dough as little as possible, to roll it out between two sheets of waxed paper, and not to worry if the crust tears; just patch it up!

3 cups all-purpose flour

½ teaspoon sea salt

1 cup solid vegetable shortening

⅓ cup butter, cold

¼ cup water

¼ cup milk

1 teaspoon freshly squeezed lemon juice

1 Combine the flour and salt in a large bowl.

2 Using two knives or a pastry blender, cut in the shortening and butter. This means you work the fats into the flour until the shortening and butter are the size of small peas.

3 In a small bowl or measuring cup, combine the water, milk, and lemon juice. Drizzle the liquid ingredients over the flour and fat mixture and combine with a fork, until the dough starts to come together.

4 With your hands, work the mixture until a dough forms. You may need to add a bit more water if the dough seems dry.

5 Divide the dough into thirds to make pie crusts that fit a 7-inch round pan. You can use the dough immediately, or shape each third of dough into a disk and put each disk into a separate freezer bag. You can freeze the dough for up to 2 months. To thaw, let stand at room temperature for an hour or two until it's workable.

6 Roll out one portion of dough between two sheets of waxed paper to form a 10-inch round circle. Use as directed in the recipe.

7 Or you can blind bake the pie crust in the air fryer. Peel off the top sheet of waxed paper. Flip it over and drape the dough over a 6- or 7-inch pie plate, then peel off the other sheet of waxed paper. Ease the dough into the pan and gently press down. Fold the edge over to make a rim and flute by pressing your fingers against the dough, working around the edge. Prick the bottom with a fork. Freeze for 20 minutes.

8 Set or preheat the air fryer to 350°F. Put the pie plate in the air fryer basket. Bake for 8 to 10 minutes or until the crust is light golden brown and set. Let cool on a rack and fill with custard, ice cream, or fresh fruit.

COOKING TIP: "Blind bake" means to bake the pie crust unfilled. To prevent the crust shrinking and puffing up in the center, line the crust with foil and add pie weights or dried beans to hold it down. Bake, then carefully remove the foil and the weights or beans.

AIR FRYER COOKING CHART

This is a general chart for reference. Your air fryer may have different cooking times and temperatures; follow the instructions that came with your appliance. Always cook foods, especially meats, poultry, and seafood, until done to a safe internal temperature.

INGREDIENT	QUANTITY	TEMPERATURE	TIME	NOTES
Broccoli, florets	2 to 4 cups	390°F	5 to 8 minutes	Lightly spray with oil; sprinkle with salt and pepper
Cauliflower, florets	2 to 4 cups	390°F	5 to 9 minutes	Mist with oil and season before frying; shake once during cooking time
Egg rolls	6 to 8	390°F	3 to 6 minutes	Brush or spray with oil before cooking
French fries, thick, fresh	2 to 4 cups	400°F	15 to 25 minutes	Lightly spray with oil
French fries, thick, frozen	2 to 4 cups	380°F	12 to 20 minutes	If there is any ice on the fries, remove it
French fries, thin, fresh	2 to 4 cups	400°F	15 to 20 minutes	Pat dry; toss with cornstarch and ½ teaspoon sugar for better browning, then mist with oil; toss once during cooking time

INGREDIENT	QUANTITY	TEMPERATURE	TIME	NOTES
French fries, thin, frozen	2 to 4 cups	390°F	10 to 14 minutes	If there is any ice clinging to the fries, remove it; toss once during cooking time
Fruit	2 to 4 cups	320°F	5 to 10 minutes for hard fruits; 3 to 5 minutes for soft fruits	Cook hard fruits, such as apples, and soft fruits, such as peaches, individually; cook hard fruits in some liquid in a pan
Muffins	4 muffins	360°F	10 to 12 minutes	Muffins should be placed inside double foil cups; place in single layer
Pizza	1 pizza	390°F	5 to 10 minutes	Place pizza on parchment paper in the basket; make sure it fits in the basket
Potatoes, chopped	4 to 7 cups	400°F	13 to 19 minutes	Spray with oil; toss once or twice during cooking time
Potatoes, sliced	4 to 5 cups	380°F	10 to 15 minutes	Slice about ⅛ inch thick; toss with oil; toss during cooking time
Potatoes, wedged	2 to 4 cups	390°F	18 to 22 minutes	Lightly spray with oil; sprinkle with salt and pepper
Sweet potatoes, cubed	4 to 6 cups	390°F	14 to 20 minutes	Lightly spray with oil

INGREDIENT	QUANTITY	TEMPERATURE	TIME	NOTES
Tofu	1 pound extra-firm, cut into cubes	400°F	10 to 15 minutes	Drain well, marinate in soy sauce, and drain again
Tofu steaks	1 to 4 steaks, cut ¾ inch thick	350°F	15 to 20 minutes	Drain tofu before grilling, cut into steaks and season before cooking
Vegetables, root	2 to 4 cups	400°F	15 to 25 minutes	Peel and cut into 1-inch chunks
Vegetables, tender	1 to 3 pounds	350°F	Sliced eggplant: 15 to 20 minutes Zucchini rounds: 10 minutes Sliced onions: 4 to 7 minutes Tomatoes: whole for 8 minutes; slices for 4 minutes Green beans: whole for 5 to 7 minutes	Cut veggies to similar sizes; cook each type of vegetable individually; shake halfway through cooking time

MEASUREMENT CONVERSIONS

	US STANDARD	US STANDARD (OUNCES)	METRIC (APPROXIMATE)
VOLUME EQUIVALENTS (LIQUID)	2 tablespoons	1 fl. oz.	30 mL
	¼ cup	2 fl. oz.	60 mL
	½ cup	4 fl. oz.	120 mL
	1 cup	8 fl. oz.	240 mL
	1½ cups	12 fl. oz.	355 mL
	2 cups or 1 pint	16 fl. oz.	475 mL
	4 cups or 1 quart	32 fl. oz.	1 L
	1 gallon	128 fl. oz.	4 L
VOLUME EQUIVALENTS (DRY)	⅛ teaspoon	————	0.5 mL
	¼ teaspoon	————	1 mL
	½ teaspoon	————	2 mL
	¾ teaspoon	————	4 mL
	1 teaspoon	————	5 mL
	1 tablespoon	————	15 mL
	¼ cup	————	59 mL
	⅓ cup	————	79 mL
	½ cup	————	118 mL
	⅔ cup	————	156 mL
	¾ cup	————	177 mL
	1 cup	————	235 mL
	2 cups or 1 pint	————	475 mL
	3 cups	————	700 mL
	4 cups or 1 quart	————	1 L
	½ gallon	————	2 L
	1 gallon	————	4 L
WEIGHT EQUIVALENTS	½ ounce	————	15 g
	1 ounce	————	30 g
	2 ounces	————	60 g
	4 ounces	————	115 g
	8 ounces	————	225 g
	12 ounces	————	340 g
	16 ounces or 1 pound	————	455 g

	FAHRENHEIT (F)	CELSIUS (C) (APPROXIMATE)
OVEN TEMPERATURES	250°F	120°C
	300°F	150°C
	325°F	180°C
	375°F	190°C
	400°F	200°C
	425°F	220°C
	450°F	230°C

RESOURCES

MANUALS

Most manuals for air fryers can be downloaded from the Web. It can be helpful to download manuals for air fryers other than the one you purchased, just for more ideas, recipes, and tips.

The manual for Philips HD9220/20 is found at p4c.philips.com/cgi-bin /cpindex.pl?ctn=HD9220/20&scy=GB&slg=ENG and includes a user manual, quick start guide, and recipe booklet.

The GLiP Oil-less Air Fryer instruction manual at homedepot.com/catalog /pdfImages/1f/1f683ead-1ebd-414d-add0-2d5a6ce0922e.pdf includes a helpful chart for cooking meats, potatoes, and snacks.

The Digital Air Fryer manual is found at belliniappliances.com.au/electrical /documents/BTDF950_U&C_140730a.pdf and includes tips on maintenance and troubleshooting, as well as a cooking chart.

The GoWISE USA Air Fryer instruction manual can be found at gowiseproducts. com/pages/owners-manuals and contains instructions for cleaning and trouble-shooting, and a cooking guide.

The Todd English Air Fryer manual is at shophq.com/images/cc/pdf /B406485TEAirFryerUPDATED.pdf and includes quite a few easy recipes.

RECIPE WEBSITES

Some other websites also have delicious and easy recipes for the air fryer.

Airfry.blogspot.com has some interesting and unusual vegetarian Indian recipes for the air fryer. They include Oats Cutlets, Banana Chips, and Cheese Spinach Balls.

Allrecipes.com/recipes/23070/everyday-cooking/cookware-and-equipment/air-fryer has lots of good recipes, including Pecan Pie Bars, Hard-Boiled Eggs, and Breakfast Frittata.

HotAirFrying.com is maintained by Philips Air Fryers. This site includes ideas for using the air fryer in new ways, along with recipes for foods such as Roasted Vegetable Pasta Salad, Air Grilled Tomatoes, and Green Curry Noodles.

PrudentPennyPincher.com/150-best-air-fryer-recipes is a great site with more than 100 recipes, including Grilled Cheese Sandwich, Baked Zucchini Fries, and Broccoli Parmesan.

RecipeThis.com/tag/airfryer-recipes has some fun recipes for this appliance. Try the Paleo Pumpkin Muffins, Fruit Crumble Mug Cakes, and Vegetable Fries.

INDEX

ABOUT THE AUTHOR

 **Linda Larsen** is an author and home economist who has been developing recipes for years. She was the Busy Cook's Guide at About.com for 15 years, writing about how to cook, food safety, and quick cooking. She has written 43 cookbooks since 2005, including *The Complete Air Fryer Cookbook* and *The Complete Slow Cooking for Two Cookbook*, as well as *Eating Clean for Dummies*. Linda has worked for the Pillsbury Company since 1988, creating and testing recipes and working for the Pillsbury Bake-Off. She holds a bachelor of arts in biology from St. Olaf College, and a bachelor of science with high distinction in food science and nutrition from the University of Minnesota. She lives in Minnesota with her husband.

Printed in the USA
CPSIA information can be obtained
at www.ICGtesting.com
LVHW052037091223
765798LV00001B/4